The Elijah Generation

Calling Men to be Prepared and to Prepare Their Families, the Church, and the World for the Coming of the Lord

By Wade McHargue

Scripture quotations are taken from the *Holy Bible, New King James Version*, Copyright © 1982 by Thomas Nelson, Inc.

Cover photo taken by Rachel Burkett

FIRST EDITION, SECOND PRINTING

ISBN: 978-1-936989-70-6

Library of Congress Control Number: 2012940817

Published by
NewBookPublishing.com, a division of Reliance Media, Inc.
515 Cooper Commerce Drive, #140, Apopka, FL 32703
NewBookPublishing.com

Printed in the United States of America

Table of Contents

Table of Contents, continued

Table of Contents, continued

Dedication

This book is dedicated to Lalas and Paulo (and thousands of others like them), men who are hungry for God and are fearlessly advancing His Kingdom in the face of persecution in the power and love of the Holy Spirit. You are running with such grace and strength; keep passing the baton and exhorting those disciples of yours to "run for the glory of God!" HalleluYah! Thank you for demonstrating to the church and world that our families can cross skin color, culture, and language and live in biblical community for the glory of God.

Preface

Behold, I will send you Elijah the prophet before the coming of the great and dreadful day of the Lord.

Malachi 4:5

First of all, it must be stated, I am not claiming to be a prophet or someone with a "special" revelation. On the contrary, I believe many will agree that the Spirit of God has already revealed to their own spirit that God is calling forth an "Elijah Generation." My prayer and burden, specifically, is that this book be a confirmation for men to answer the call, to rise up and take their place in this "Elijah Generation." I am praying that this will be read by those whom God directs to do so, and that it will be a clarion call, a blast, a battle cry to fight the good fight, to throw off the old man and his deeds, to bring forth the fruits of repentance, and to press towards the prize, the high calling in Christ Jesus.

The present issue and need for the Church is for His Word to be allowed to penetrate our hearts that we might receive true

Holy Spirit revelation (1 Corinthians 2:10-16) of the character and glory of God, of His standard and expectation, of the inheritance and promises we have in Christ, and of the burden of the Spirit to "go and make disciples of every nation."

That is why it is my hope that the attention and emphasis of this book is concerning His Word and drawing attention to what I believe is His specific Word, His "rhema," in this hour. However, I also acknowledge the power of current testimonies and how much they encourage me (and others). That is why the testimonies in this book for the most part are not "borrowed" from those who lived years ago (although we give God glory for their testimonies!) Rather, they are personal experiences of our living God. I pray that they will strengthen your faith as you give glory to God with me. I hope even some will feel led to write me their testimonies that I too may be strengthened in my faith and walk with God.

Secondly, I want it to be understood that any profit that this book receives above the cost of publishing, printing, packaging, shipping and handling, etc., will be given toward world evangelism and the persecuted church. Even the thought of making a personal profit from this book is out of the question to me and would be completely contrary to the message of the book. I know more than ever just how wealthy I am as an American and how much I can live without. I, myself, am trying to live the reality I have written about in Chapter 24 of this book. This truth has been confirmed to me even more after having lived overseas for years in a country like Guinea Bissau, which is rated by the United Nations and other agencies as one of the top five poorest countries in the world. Money needs to pour out from God's people for the purposes of the Kingdom, not for personal gain of wealth and possessions. I would go further than this in saying I believe less money should remain in America and more be sent into the *10/40 window where the greatest need is. People are dying and going to hell without Jesus, and many national (indigenous) pastors and missionaries are severely limited, living on little, not knowing where they will get their next meal let alone even thinking about "retirement," a word not even in the hearts of these servants. I know, because I have met some of them. May God use this book to get His money into the hands of those He wants to receive it for the preaching of His Gospel and the glorification of His Son.

This book is really the result of two life-changing encounters I have had with God.

While I lived in Charlotte, North Carolina, I was part of "Jackson Park Ministries," a wonderful ministry which reaches out to the poor, the addicted, the single parent, and struggling families in order to see them equipped to get out of debt, to know how to work biblically together as a family, and to walk in the new life in Christ. For more info, please visit their website at www.jacksonpark.org. The leadership of the ministry graciously let me use the facility to host a gathering of men who came for three days to receive teaching from an elder brother in the Lord (we were blessed to have Dr. Michael Brown), to receive teaching from other brothers in Christ, and to spend extended time seeking God's face in worship and prayer. We then would go out two-by-two, evangelizing in a rough area of Charlotte and bringing the Kingdom of heaven to earth. None of these men came with the purpose of having merely a "holy huddle." They were ready to go out and be "doers" of the Word and not just merely "hearers." It was during the second year of such a gathering (we met annually during New Year's weekend) that I had the first of these two specific life-changing encounters.

After an evening of evangelistic outreach, we reunited in

the chapel at JPM to testify of the great things God had done: the souls that had surrendered to Jesus and those who had been healed or delivered in His Name. After a time of teaching, all the men began singing a capella, (we were a little off-key, but the Lord received our worship!) We sang songs of the blood of Jesus, hymns like "Nothing But the Blood of Jesus" and "There Is Power in the Blood."

Suddenly the power and presence of God fell upon us. I do not believe any of us were expecting God to reveal Himself at that moment, but each man was ushered into His holy presence. I was overcome and began trembling all over as I felt this deep cry within me beginning to mount in intensity. I remember speaking within to God, "Not now, Lord. What will these brothers think?" To which God quickly responded, "Why are you so concerned with what they think? Let Me have My way."

Immediately, as I surrendered, a cry came out of me that I cannot adequately describe. The men who were there that night can attest to that moment. I, myself, did not know what I was crying out at first—it was a deep belly cry as a woman cries out in the midst of childbirth. Then the Holy Spirit helped me give articulation, "O, God! Forgive us! Forgive us! You are Holy! You are Holy! We have sinned against You; we have grieved You! Raise up Your army, O God!!! For You are worthy!"

Until that moment in my life I have never, as it is referred to, "fallen out" or being "slain" in the Spirit, which many have experienced by the laying on of hands. Never. And I have had hands laid on me by many men of God who often witness this. But that night in the chapel I fell so hard I had an imprint of the carpet on my cheek. I lay there for three hours as I felt the fire of God going up and down my chest. I felt as though I weighed ten thousand pounds.

I cried and cried until this tremendous sense of cleansing came over me. I finally felt God releasing me from this great burden. It was a burden for God's church, specifically the men of the church, to throw off sin and to walk in holiness, abandonment, and faithful love for and towards Jesus in all areas of life. The Lord dealt strongly with me to show me the intensity of His holiness, the sacredness of his Son's blood, the compromise in the church, and His great desire to see his children walk with Him. I understand that the word "glory" in Hebrew literally means "weight." I can assure you that is what I had experienced. It changed my life. Every man in that room also encountered God in a life-changing way.

The second such life-changing encounter with God occurred in 2008, also at Jackson Park Ministry. With permission from JPM, some of the men from the yearly gathering had begun a weekly Friday night service in the chapel. It was an outreach effort working with the students from F.I.R.E. School of Ministry, located north of Charlotte in Concord, North Carolina.

One night, as a brother was leading worship, I fell to my knees. With my face to the ground I felt the presence of God come strongly upon me. I began to feel the fire of God again, a burning sensation in my heart, and He began to speak very clearly to me and show me visions of what He was doing. I heard Him speak that I was to be among many who would be a part of the "Elijah Generation." I was told to go back and to study the lives of Elijah and John the Baptist, who came in the spirit of Elijah (Luke 1:17). I was to be a part of the mobilization of men who would also answer this call.

In obedience, I began studying the lives of Elijah and John the Baptist and the prophecy concerning the coming of Elijah. I believe the Spirit of God drew my attention to thirty specific characteristics found in this study. Today, after almost five years since this experience, the message has not lessened but has intensified into a focused, consuming call. I believe God has called me to write down what He has sealed and confirmed in my spirit. Again, I believe this book will also be a confirmation in the hearts of many who have sensed this same call. As I have preached this message, I have heard testimonies from men whose spirits gave exceptionally strong witness that this word resonates within as truth. They/we are in one accord.

If this is the work of the Holy Spirit, it will bear fruit and will remain as a witness in the hearts of God's people—rather than being a passing emotional phase to serve as the platform for some "pep rally." Time will reveal what will stand, what will endure.

Introduction

Help, Lord, for the godly man ceases! For the faithful disappear from among the sons of men.

Psalms 12:1

One thing that can be noted clearly from Scriptures is that God uses men! He used men to preach righteousness in the midst of an ungodly generation as early as Enoch (Jude 14-15). He used men to whom He entrusted His covenants, as Abraham (Genesis 12). He used men to stir up slumbering nations as He did through such prophets as Isaiah, Jeremiah, and Ezekiel. He used and is using men to take the Gospel of Jesus Christ to the nations. Does God use women powerfully as well? Of course! However, the specific reason I felt led by the Spirit to write this book is to address the men of the church. This is my passion and burden.

God wants to use men, and it should come as no surprise that Satan would, therefore, make this a focus of attack. "So goes the man," so goes the potential great influence upon his wife, his children (and subsequently, the next generation), the Church, and the fulfillment of the Great Commission.

God is calling you, Brother, to rise up, heed His call, and walk with Him, preparing the way for the coming of the LORD! I encourage you, as you read each of the thirty characteristics of an Elijah (perhaps focusing on just one a day), to not only meditate on them but also to pray and to declare the truth of them into your very life, in Jesus Name. A the end of every six chapters there are also discussion questions and points of application for those wanting to do this as a men's group study. This is to divide the book into a five-week study, which I pray would result in an organized outreach at the end of the time.

O Lord God, let the Elijah Generation arise!!!

"You have not because you ask not." (James 4:2b)

"Until now you have asked nothing in my name: ask, and you will receive, that your joy may be full." (John 16:24)

CHAPTER 1

Elijah, a Prophetic Voice for Holiness in a Time of Immorality

And it came to pass, as though it had been a trivial thing for him to walk in the sins of Jeroboam the son of Nebat, that he took as wife Jezebel the daughter of Ethbaal, king of the Sidonians, and he went and served Baal and worshiped him. Then he set up an altar for Baal in the temple of Baal, which he had built in Samaria. And Ahab made a wooden image. Ahab did more to provoke the LORD God of Israel to anger than all the kings of Israel who were before him.

1 Kings 16:31-33

"Nevertheless I have a few things against you, because you allow that woman Jezebel, who calls herself a prophetess, to teach and seduce My servants to commit sexual immorality and eat things sacrificed to idols. And I gave her time to

repent of her sexual immorality, and she did not
repent. Indeed I will cast her into a sickbed, and
those who commit adultery with her into great
tribulation, unless they repent of their deeds. I will
kill her children with death, and all the churches
shall know that I am He who searches the minds
and hearts. And I will give to each one of you
according to your works."

Revelation 2:20-23

Elijah (whose name means "My God is Yahweh") is first mentioned in 1 Kings 17. Does it not catch your attention, the "suddenness" of his appearing? There is no mention of his family background or younger years. I believe God is speaking that even in these last days He is raising up men, many of whom may never have expected to be among those being called by the Spirit. They have nothing "special" about their past or family background. In fact, they very well may represent the first generation of believers in their family. They are among those who will suddenly "appear" with the anointing of God to declare the Word of the Lord. Praise God for those who have been given the inheritance of a godly family lineage for generations. But praise God, also, that God is a God Who is no respecter of persons, and He will use everyone and anyone who is completely surrendered to Him. So, Brother, throw off the lie and any thought that you are disqualified or unqualified because of your background or your past. The blood of Jesus is enough. Stop wallowing in self-condemnation. There is no victory in that. God is not glorified in that. It is time to stop letting the devil beat you up. It is time get up and believe the promise of God that if you confess your sins He is faithful and just to forgive you your sins and cleanse you from all unrighteousness (1 John 1:9).

However, we must remember that confession is to lead to repentance. Stop falling on your face in defeat if God is saying to you as He did to Joshua, "Get up! Why do you lie thus on your face? Israel has sinned, and they have also transgressed My covenant which I commanded them. For they have even taken some of the accursed things, and have both stolen and deceived; and they have also put it among their own stuff. Therefore, the children of Israel could not stand before their enemies..." (Joshua 7:10-12).

It is time to deal with the sin in our lives! If there are "accursed things" in our hearts and in our homes then it is time to get them out and stop walking around trying to fool ourselves into thinking there are no consequences to what we welcome into our hearts and homes.

Take to heart the account of Phinehas. God had judged Israel for their intermarrying with the pagans. They had already witnessed God's anger when they saw the leaders killed for their sin. Now here in Numbers 25 we read of a man coming boldly with a pagan woman to commit sin in the eyes of everyone. What did most of them do in response? Nothing, which sadly is the same testimony of too many today. The people watched and wept—all except Phinehas, that is. Phinehas arose in righteous anger and, taking up a spear, entered the sinners' tent. While possibly in the very act of their sexual immorality, righteous Phinehas pinned them both to the ground with his spear!

How did God respond to this? Did He say, "Phinehas, you didn't have to do that!" or, perhaps, "Calm down, Phinehas!" No!!! Hear the Word of God!

"Phinehas the son of Eleazer, the son of Aaron the priest, has turned back My wrath from the children of Israel, because he was zealous <u>with My zeal</u> among them, so that I did not consume the children of Israel in My zeal. Therefore say, 'Behold, I give to him <u>My covenant of peace</u>; and it shall be <u>to him and his descendants</u> after him a covenant of an everlasting priesthood, <u>because he was zealous for his God</u>, and made atonement for the children of Israel'" (Numbers 25:11-13).

Phinehas mirrored the zeal of God! He would not only be blessed but so would his descendants! This is God speaking!

We know that God many times will reveal the physical first to help bring further spiritual understanding and revelation later. For us who live under the New Covenant and walk in the Spirit we know the war is spiritual. Nevertheless, the principle remains. <u>Deal violently with that sin!</u> Take the sword of the Spirit, the Word of God, and pin it to the ground! Do not just stand there! That vile, ungodly thing is going to destroy you and bring the discipline and judgment of Almighty God! I am amazed at the false teaching being embraced by so many, and have actually heard a sermon (from a respected church among many Spirit-filled believers) declaring that believers cannot be punished and will not receive consequences for their actions! Beware of those who do not preach the full counsel of God! The apostle Peter declares that <u>judgment</u> will begin <u>in the house of God, not in the world!</u> (1 Peter 4:17) and Paul says we will reap what we sow (Galatians 6:7,8). How anyone can teach that God will not judge His church in light of Revelation chapter 2 and 3 is a wonder. Paul talks clearly of even the <u>church's</u> responsibility to discipline and judge those in the church who are walking in sin as he states in 1 Corinthians 5. What relevance would any of Paul's warnings have then to the church in his epistles if one embraces this "hyper grace" message? The language of the New Testament is clear, Brother. By the Spirit, we are to "put to death the deeds of the body" (Romans 8:13). I ask you, how much clearer can it get?

What was the context of Elijah's appearing? It was during the reign of King Ahab.

1. It was the man of God coming against the man of compromise.

2. It was the man of the Spirit coming against the man of the flesh.

3. It was the Spirit of the world-to-come against the spirit of this world.

4. It was the man of order, Elijah, coming against the man out-of-order, Ahab, who allowed his wife Jezebel to have the final authority over their household because of his spiritual compromise. It was during the time when the principle god of the land was Baal, the god of fertility and the god of sex, whose followers would "worship" by fornicating on a hill under a green tree. It was under the rule of Jezebel, the woman who epitomized the lust of the eyes, the lust of the flesh, and the pride of life. She was a woman of manipulation, a woman with a controlling spirit, a woman used by the enemy to seduce God's people to sexual sin and to reverse God's order of marriage and the home.*

It was Jezebel who was Elijah's chief enemy. It was Delilah who Sampson allowed to seduce him, sapping his anointing and leaving him blind and weak and an object of mocking and derision. Hear the warning from God's Word Brother! It was Potiphar's wife seeking to seduce Joseph but failing. It was Herodias, in that similar spirit of Jezebel, that was the one fighting the prophetic words of John the Baptist, "Prepare the way for the Lord!" [And it was Jesus' words of warning to the church of Thyatira in Revelation 2 against their tolerating Jezebel in their midst, allowing her to seduce God's servants to fornicate. God will not be silent!]

And so here we are today. What is crippling the church? Where are the men of God? Where has their authority gone? We are living during the reign of Ahab again, and Jezebel roams the land calling for the worship of Baal. In America, pornography is an annual billion dollar industry. Christian organizations are saying some 93% of young men have been exposed to porn before 18 years of age, and the majority of those exposed become ensnared and enslaved. "Christian men" have been so numbed by the god of this world that they think little anymore of what is darkening their minds every single day (and many times what they purposely expose themselves to). How true are the words of Proverbs about this sin, "For she has cast down many wounded, and all who were slain by her were strong men" (Proverbs 7:26), and by such sin "a man is reduced to a crust of bread; and an adulteress will hunt for the precious life" (Proverb 4:26).

How far do we have to go, Brother, to call compromise what it really is? It's sin. "The backslider in heart will be filled with his own ways, but a good man will be satisfied from above" (Proverb 14:14). Do you really think that junk on the Internet will satisfy you or bring about God's blessings and desire for your life? Do you need to see that television program that is filled with lewd comments and sexual innuendos? The commercials by themselves are an affront to God, and are you welcoming that into your home? How many believers do you know who have their bookshelf filled with movies that have scenes of sex or with women scantily dressed or making references to sex? If you say that this does not affect you, then you have become calloused to sin. That is not a sign of spiritual maturity but of compromise. The Holy Spirit is the Holy Spirit and He hates and is grieved what someone may say they are "indifferent" to or what they say is covered under "grace." The Holy Spirit still is just as holy as He ever was or ever will be. He DOES NOT change.

It is time. It is time to be angry at how sin has ravaged the church—specifically, the men of the church. It is time be angry at how this sin has destroyed marriages and the innocence of children. The command of God is to be angry but not to sin in that anger (Ephesians 4:26). There is a righteous anger against sin and the works of the devil. That anger should move you to action. The world is lost, dead in its sin, but, Brother, you and I know better—if we are claiming to be the temple of the Holy Spirit, new creations, and children of light. There are no excuses. God says, "Come out from among them and be separate, says the Lord. Do not touch what is unclean, and I will receive you. I will be a Father to you. And you shall be My sons and daughters, says the Lord Almighty" (2 Corinthians 6:17-18, emphasis mine). It is time to take on the spirit of Phinehas and pin this sin to the ground and get the garbage out of your home and out of your heart. You must do it for the glory of God, for the sake of Jesus, and for the love of the Holy Spirit. You must do it for your sake, your wife's (or future wife's) sake, and for your children's sake, that they might walk in that inheritance and blessing of God. God's Word is clear, "The fear of the Lord is the hatred of evil" (Romans 8:13). To love what God loves is to hate what He hates. "Abhor what is evil. Cling to what is good." are the words of God (Romans 12:9, Amos 5:15). It is time to really invite Jesus into our homes.

In America in the past, backsliding was recognized by the neglect of the family altar.

"Family altar? That sounds archaic."

No, Brother, that is what God expects. It was the model of the patriarchs and the command of God (Deuteronomy 6:7). The family altar in early America was not just a table with an opened Bible nor, usually, the first thing you saw or noticed coming into a home. (By the way, if it is your home, or rather should it not be said, if it is to be His home, do not even consider believing the lie of the enemy that you do not want to come across as "super spiritual" and that you would rather pacify unsaved neighbors or friends, being more concerned about what they might think than about simply being a man of principle and conviction. Unfortunately, many of our churches model their services in this same mindset, i.e. for the unsaved and not the saved.) The family altar was the place the fathers led their families in family devotions, Scripture reading, prayer, and worship at least once a day. It was a place where the family came together to consecrate themselves and declare the Lordship of Jesus over their lives. It was a time, as a family, of meeting with God.

Do you have a family altar? Perhaps you do, but is it of God?

It was Anton LaVey, the co-founder of the church of Satan, who recognized that along with music, television would be used to destroy Christians and families. He said, "The birth of the TV was a magical event foreshadowing its satanic significance.... Since then, TV's infiltration has been so gradual, so complete, that no one even noticed. People don't need to go to church any more; they get their morality plays on television. The TV set, or satanic family altar, has grown more elaborate since the early 50's, from the tiny fuzzy screen to huge entertainment centers, covering entire walls with several TV monitors. What started as a innocent respite from everyday life has become in itself a replacement for real life for millions, a major religion for the masses" (Devil's Notebook, 1992, pg. 86).

The writer of a famous television show said, "If we can get the people laughing, they will accept things not normally acceptable, and we can slip our message under the door."

"If we can get the people laughing..."

What are you laughing at friend? What do you find funny?

Please do not use the excuse you are too busy and that is why you do not have a family altar for Jesus. If you keep an eternal perspective, you will make time. You would be amazed how much time you spend on things that can be cut back. A brother in Christ led a group of fellow missionaries, including myself and men who had a heart for more of God in New York City, in a revealing exercise at a meeting at the Brooklyn Tabernacle. We were asked to break down how we use our time hourly. Do the exercise — this week if you can. Break down a 168-hour week and see how you are spending your time and how you can redeem it for God and for your family. Men, it is time to rise up and establish the family altar again, removing the television from its place as the central object of the home. Let us be men who are leading our families in discipleship through the Word, in heart-felt worship, and in prayer!

It is time that we as the Church stop allowing Jezebel into our homes and into our hearts. Shut off the television and give yourself to seeking the face of God. Do not be a victim of the reign of Jezebel or a participant with the worshipers of Baal. Instead, be a prophetic voice against these things. When this happens the men of the church will have influence, rather than being influenced. Men will speak up and stop allowing their sons and daughters to dress and act like the world. Men will oppose the entrance of the world's values into the church by speaking out in loving opposition. The "spirit" of Ahab has been around too long.

It begins with you and me, Brother.

Father, we ask You to reveal any compromise in our hearts and anywhere that we have tolerated Jezebel in our lives or homes. As You reveal these things to us, we will destroy them without delay. Delay is not of You, for delayed obedience is disobedience. Let us now begin to establish the family altar in a spirit of love and humility, not to fulfill some religious duty, but to meet with You, to encounter You, and to give You the preeminence You deserve in our lives, in Jesus Name.

CHAPTER 2

Elijah, a Man Who Knew the Voice of God and Spoke the Word of God with Boldness

*And Elijah the Tishbite, of the inhabitants of
Gilead, said to Ahab, "As the LORD God of Israel
lives, before whom I stand, there shall not be dew
nor rain these years, except at my word."*

1 Kings 17:1

*Then He said, "Go out, and stand on the mountain
before the LORD." And behold, the LORD passed
by, and a great and strong wind tore into the
mountains and broke the rocks in pieces before the
LORD, but the LORD was not in the wind; and
after the wind an earthquake, but the LORD was
not in the earthquake; and after the earthquake a
fire, but the LORD was not in the fire; and after the*

*fire a still small voice. So it was, when Elijah heard
it, that he wrapped his face in his mantle and went
out and stood in the entrance of the cave. Suddenly
a voice called unto him, and said, "What are you
doing here, Elijah?"*

1 Kings 19:11-13

Men, we are to know the voice of God. So why do so many
not hear clearly the voice of God? How do you know the
voice of God? First and foremost, it is by the Word of God. This is
not just doing a five-minute devotional or depending on others to
constantly feed you like a newborn baby; it is time to grow up and
be men who have moved from milk to meat and know how to feed
themselves!

We, as the Church, need to repent of just plain laziness. While
living in West Africa, I was amazed at the way the Muslims there
would commit large portions of the Koran to memory in Arabic,
which is not their first language. How is it the people of God, who
have the help of the Spirit of God, who have the very words of God,
have hardly any of the Word memorized in their heart language? Is
it any wonder then that so few men walk in spiritual authority and
victory? When you are in the day of battle, you do not say to your
enemy, "Hold on, let me run back and get my weapons. I'll be right
back." No! You are ready! You have the Sword already in your
mouth; there is not time to run back in the moment of temptation!
We, the Church, need to repent of laziness and we must understand
the centrality of the Word. We are meant to be like Joshua and take
the land for the Kingdom of God just like the early church did in the

power and character of the Holy Spirit. But what were his marching orders? What would be the key to his success?

"This Book of the Law shall not depart from your mouth, but you shall meditate in it day and night, that you may observe to do according to all that is written in it. For then you will make your way prosperous, and then you will have good success" (Joshua 1:8, emphasis mine). David knew this too, "But his delight is in the law of the LORD, and in His law he meditates day and night. He shall be like a tree planted by the rivers of water, that brings forth its fruit in its season, whose leaf also shall not wither; and whatever he does shall prosper" (Psalms 1:2-3).

To be a man in the Jewish culture was synonymous with knowing the Word of God and having large portions of it memorized. We must return to our Jewish roots, Brothers! It is time to do this ourselves and expect it of our children. How else can they keep their way clean in the midst of a crooked and perverse generation (Psalms 119:9, 11)? The bar has to be raised from "Jesus loves me, this I know."

We must return to knowing that the Word is to be central in our lives.

I encourage you to meditate and say out loud the following:

1. The Word gives me faith (Romans 10:17).
2. The Word gives me the ability to resist sin (Psalms 119:11).
3. The Word prospers me, as God defines prosperity (Joshua 1:8, Psalm 1:3)!
4. The Word expands, broadens, and deepens my worship of God (John 4:24).
5. The Word shows me that I am a true disciple of Jesus if I remain in it (John 8:31).

6. The Word leads me to freedom (John 8:32).

7. The Word makes me fruitful in my life (Mark 4:3, 14).

8. The Word brings conviction and revelation (Hebrews 4:12,13).

9. The Word brings answered prayer according to His will (John 15:7).

10. The Word sanctifies me (John 17:17).

11. The Word empowers me for spiritual warfare (Ephesians 6:10-18, 1 John 2:14, 2 Corinthians 10:3-5).

12. The Word gives understanding of my inheritance in Christ (Ephesians 1:14-19, Romans 8:10-17).

13. The Word gives me godly counsel in day-to-day living (Proverbs).

14. The Word is my spiritual food—needed daily! (Matthew 4:4, Hebrews 5:12-14, 1 Peter 2:2).

15. The Word of God is Jesus Christ, and thus reading it is the way for me to get to know Him (John 1, Revelation 19:11-13).

16. The Word brings healing (Psalm 107:20).

17. The Word is to be my delight (Psalm 119:47, 97, 162).

18. The Word makes me wise beyond my experience and years (Psalm 119:97-100, Proverbs 1:1-6, 1:20-25).

19. The Word gives me guidance (Psalm 119:105, 133).

20. The Word is what was used to bring me into salvation, and it **prepares** me for the world to come because it is eternal—for the things of this world are passing away (Psalm 12:7, 1 Peter 1:23-25)!

It is time to stop making excuses and start memorizing the Word of God. Memorization is inseparable from meditation. Start today, Brother. God will honor you and He has promised that the Holy Spirit will help you (John 14:26). If the Muslims can do it without the Spirit of God, then surely we can memorize the Word of God in our heart language with the help of the power of the Spirit of God!

The priests of old had blood put on their ear and on their thumb and on their big toe (Leviticus 8:23-24). God reveals the physical first, then the spiritual. We are His priests (1 Peter 2:9), called to have the blood of Jesus applied to our ears to hear the voice of God! It is God's will that we hear His voice! "My sheep hear My voice, and I know them, and they follow Me" (John 10:27). This is not for some spiritual "elite," but it is the blessing and privilege of every son of God. Take hold of the promise and throw off the lies of Satan that say you are not worthy or you are just this or just that. If you are His sheep, then it applies to you. Our standard is to be the Bible, not anything else, and according to the Bible, the early church knew the voice of the Spirit (for examples, see Acts 13:2; 15:27 28; 16:6; 20:23,28). It is by knowing God's voice through knowing His Word that we walk in spiritual authority and are then able to speak the Word of God with boldness and confidence. Those who kneel before God can stand before anyone. As Leonard Ravenhill once said, "Those who are intimate with God, are not intimidated by anyone." We ought to speak boldly in love to anyone, whether a pauper or a president, not giving consideration to a man's wealth, position, or prestige, but only to the Father in Heaven.

How the enemy loves to fill our minds and our ears with distractions, preoccupations, and just plain noise. When we quiet ourselves, shut off the noise and images of this world, and discipline ourselves to stay at His feet, we will find, like Mary, that we have "chosen the better part" (Luke 10:42). It is by the renewing of the mind, by giving ourselves to meditating on and memorizing His Word that we can discern the good, acceptable, and perfect will of God (Romans 12:2). Brothers, we must renew our minds—starting now! This means shutting off the garbage and cutting off the feeding tube of this world from our lives. Starve your flesh! It is time to feed your spirit with the Word of God, our spiritual food. It is time to get acquainted with the voice of God.

"For as he thinks in his heart, so is he" (Proverbs 23:7).

What we think about, what we stay our minds on is what reveals who we really are. We are called to walk with a clean conscience (Acts 24:16).

It is from this renewed mind that true boldness arises, for you know that if God is for you, who can be against you? (Romans 8:35). You would rather be with God in the minority than be found against God in the majority. It is the righteous who are bold as a lion (Proverbs 28:1). Do not walk around like an Ahab, weak, cowardly, a victim of the spirit of lust and sexual sin. Stop setting what is wicked before your eyes! (See Psalm 101:3). Be filled with His boldness, His life, and His victory as you renew your mind in the Word of God. Again, it was the source of success for Joshua (Joshua 1:8, 9) and David (Psalm 1, 119) and is the mark of a true disciple of Jesus (John 8:31). By the Word, renew your mind! I implore you again in the Name of Jesus, start memorizing the Word today! If you haven't already begun memorizing the Word, see Appendix A for a list of Scriptures you can begin using. Then you will make disciples who will do the same, starting with your wife and kids.

Father, we ask for forgiveness on behalf of ourselves and the church of America for overall laziness and not hiding Your Word in our hearts. Lord, expose any excuses, any lies we've believed from the enemy who has fought so hard to keep Your sons from memorizing Your holy Word. May we follow the example of Jesus as He showed us the victory over Satan in the wilderness as we, too, declare the Word of God, the sword of the Spirit. Help us, O God! Spirit of God, we invite You to hold us accountable. Thank You for empowering us to memorize the Word and thank You for the revelation You are going to bring, for we know the Word must be spiritually discerned. We ask for forgiveness for the cowardice in Your church. Let us ask for boldness just as Your early church did in Acts 4 and Paul did in Ephesians 6. Give us boldness Father, in Jesus Name!

CHAPTER 3

Elijah, a Man of Obedience

So he went and did according unto the word of the LORD, for he went and stayed by the Brook Cherith, which flows into the Jordan.
1 Kings 17:5

Some may point out that they already have a lot of Scripture memorized but still have difficulty hearing God's voice. A prophet of the Lord said the question he was most frequently asked was, "What is the secret of hearing God's voice?" He replied that if you have the intention to obey what God will tell you before He speaks, you will never lack for hearing God's voice. Read that one again. The simplicity of his answer was a sign to me that it was of God, because it is man who complicates the subject of hearing God's voice, trying to sound sophisticated and philosophical.

The problem is that too many want God to speak, but they think that obedience is optional. The reason you are not filled with joy, Brother, may be that you have not obeyed what God has already told you to do. Why would He speak to you again if you have not obeyed what He has already told you to do? I am asking the Holy Spirit to bring to your mind anything that He has already told you to do but you have not yet obeyed. If He reveals something you have neglected to obey, put this book down and go do it— now. Nothing is more important. He wants you to be in fellowship with Him! He loves you!

Obedience is the mark of the child of God. The word "obey" is first mentioned in the Bible in the same chapter that "worship" and "love" are first mentioned, Genesis 22. The context (and personal application) of this passage is taking that which is most precious to you and being willing to sacrifice it for God, showing that He has preeminence in your life and that you follow/obey Him without reservation.

God rebuked Saul by stating clearly through Samuel, "To obey is better than sacrifice, and to heed than the fat of rams" (1 Samuel 15:22). In fact, in this same passage God said rebellion was as the sin of <u>witchcraft</u> and stubbornness of heart like <u>idolatry</u>.

1. Obedience is why God established His promises with men.

And the LORD said, "Shall I hide from Abraham what I am doing, since Abraham shall surely become a great and mighty nation, and all the nations of the earth shall be blessed in him? For I have known him, in order <u>that he may command his children and his household after him, that keep the way of the LORD, to do righteousness and justice, that the LORD may bring to Abraham what He has spoken to him</u> (Genesis 18:17-19, emphasis mine).

And I will make your descendants multiply as the stars of heaven; I will give to your descendants all these lands; and in your seed shall the nations of the earth shall be blessed; <u>because</u> Abraham obeyed My voice and kept My charge, My commandments, My statutes, and My laws (Genesis 26:4-5, emphasis mine).

2.   Obedience is what makes way for God's prosperity and blessing.

Only be strong and very courageous, that you may observe to do according to all the law which Moses My servant commanded you: do not turn from it to the right hand or to the left, that you may prosper wherever you go (Joshua 1:7, emphasis mine).

So if you walk in My ways, to keep My statutes and My commandments, as your father David walked, then I will lengthen your days (1 Kings 3:14, emphasis mine).

3.   Disobedience brings God's judgment and discipline.

Therefore the LORD was very angry with Israel, and removed them from his sight; there was none left but the tribe of Judah alone. Also Judah did not keep the commandments of the LORD their God, but walked in the statutes of Israel which they made. And the LORD rejected all the descendants of Israel, afflicted them, and delivered them into the hand of plunderers, until He had cast them from His sight (2 Kings 17:18-20).

"One who turns away his ear from hearing the law, even his prayer is an abomination" (Proverbs 28:9).

Therefore prepare yourself and arise, and speak to them all that I command you. Do not be dismayed before their faces, lest I dismay you before them (Jeremiah 1:17).

"Now these things became our examples, to the intent that we should not lust after evil things as they also lusted (1 Corinthians 10:6)

And you have forgotten the exhortation which speaks to you as to sons: "My son, do not despise the chastening of the LORD, nor be discouraged when you are rebuked by Him; for whom the LORD loves he chastens, and scourges every son whom He receives." If you endure chastening, God deals with you as with sons; for what son is there whom a father does not chasten? But if you are without chastening, of which all have become partakers, then you are illegitimate bastards and not sons. Furthermore, we have had human fathers who corrected us, and we paid them respect. Shall we not much more readily be in subjection to the Father of spirits and live? For they indeed for a few days chastened us as seemed best to them, but he for our profit, that we may be partakers of His holiness. Now no chastening seems to be joyful for the present, but painful; nevertheless, afterward it yields the peaceable fruit of righteousness to those who have been trained by it (Hebrews 12:5-11).

4. Obedience could be an issue of life and death.

When I say to the wicked, 'You shall surely die,' and you give him no warning, nor speak to warn the wicked from his wicked way, to save his life, that same wicked man shall die in his iniquity; but his blood I will require at your hand. Yet if you warn the wicked, and he does not turn from his wickedness, nor from his wicked way, he shall die in his iniquity; but you have delivered your soul (Ezekiel 3:18-19).

5. Obedience should be motivated by love, but it is also biblical for it to be motivated by a fear of God.

See that you do not refuse Him who speaks. For if they did not escape who refused Him who spoke on earth, much more shall we not escape if we turn away from Him who speaks from heaven, whose voice then shook the earth; but now He has promised, saying,

"Yet once more I shake not only the earth, but also heaven. Now this, "Yet once more," indicates the removal of those things that are being shaken, as of things that are made, that the things which cannot be shaken may remain. Therefore, since we are receiving a kingdom which cannot be shaken, let us have grace, by which we may serve God acceptably with reverence and godly fear. For our God is a consuming fire (Heb 12:25-29, emphasis mine).

6. Obedience reveals whether we are servants of sin or of righteousness.

"What then? Shall we sin because we are not under the law, but under grace? Certainly not! Do you not know that to whom you present yourselves slaves to obey, you are that one's slaves whom you obey, whether of sin leading to death, or of obedience leading to righteousness?" (Romans 6:15-16).

7. Obedience starts with our thought life and its being submitted to God.

"For the weapons of our warfare are not carnal but mighty in God for pulling down strongholds, casting down arguments and every high thing that exalts itself against the knowledge of God, bringing every thought into captivity to the obedience of Christ, and being ready to punish all disobedience when your obedience is fulfilled" (2 Corinthians 10:4-6).

8. Obedience is connected to a life that is sanctified and separated from the world's lusts.

"Therefore gird up the loins of your mind, be sober, and rest your hope fully upon the grace that is to be brought to you at the revelation of Jesus Christ; as obedient children, not conforming yourselves to the former lusts, as in your ignorance; but as He who called you is holy, you also be holy in all your conduct, because it is written, "Be holy, for I am holy" (1 Peter 1:14-16).

9. Obedience is learned, as it was with Jesus, through the fire of tribulation.

"Though He was a Son, yet He learned obedience by the things which He suffered" (Hebrews 5:8).

10. Obedience is what will reveal if we really know Jesus and if He is truly the Lord of our lives.

"But why do you call Me 'Lord, Lord,' and not do the things which I say?" (Luke 6:46).

"If anyone loves Me, he will keep My word; and My Father will love him, and We will come to him and make Our home with him" (John 14:23).

11. Obedience is how God declares our love is shown to Him.

"If you love Me, keep My commandments" (John 14:15). Our Father feels loved not just by our singing songs about how we love Him, but by our living in obedience to His Word. Consequently, Jesus clearly says that those who do not keep His Word do not love Him (John 14:24)!

12. Obedience is how we come into greater revelations of God.

"He who has My commandments and keeps them, it is he who loves Me. And he who loves Me will be loved by My Father, and I will love him and manifest Myself to him" (John 14:21).

Obedience is not optional. Many have tried to dichotomize the God of the Old Testament from the God of the New, and thus make the argument that "we are not under Law but grace." If by this they mean we have more liberty to sin and get away with it, they are wrong. God does give us time to repent, but do not be deceived; He is the same God. Now that we are under the New Covenant with the Holy Spirit of God living in us, how much more does He expect obedience! Brothers, this is a very serious issue. We must return to the Word of God and what it clearly states. We must beware of depending solely on teachers and not on the Teacher (John 14:26). The Word "grace" is not just used in the context of salvation given by God (e.g., Ephesians 2:8-9), but also as God's empowerment to fulfill what He expects and commands of us (Romans 12:6, 15:15, 1 Corinthians 15:10, 2 Corinthians 9:8, 12:9, Ephesians 3:7, 4:7, 2 Timothy 2:1, Hebrews 4:16, 1 Peter 4:10, 2 Peter 3:18). This includes walking in holiness. Grace is not something to be abused but something we are to be growing in! This false teaching that somehow God is more "lax" concerning obedience and following His commandments can be shut down with just one familiar passage of scripture from the New Testament:

For if we sin willfully after we have received the knowledge of the truth, there no longer remains a sacrifice for sins, but a certain fearful expectation of judgment, and fiery indignation which will devour the adversaries. Anyone who has rejected Moses' law dies without mercy on the testimony of two or three witnesses. **Of how much worse punishment,** do you suppose will he be thought worthy who has trampled the Son of God underfoot, counted the blood of the covenant by which he was sanctified a common thing, and insulted the Spirit of grace? For we know Him who said, "Vengeance is Mine, I will repay", says the Lord. And again, "The Lord will judge His people. It is a fearful thing to fall into the hands of the living God (Heb 10:26-31).

Jesus actually raised the bar not lowered it (Matthew 5-7). He revealed that God requires righteousness within our hearts and how God is looking at our motivation of *why* we do what we do and not just *what* we do.

It is time to obey, to surrender all, and to walk with God.

Remember, *obedience* = *love* in the eyes of God, and *love* = *obedience*.

The Hebrew and Greek words translated as "spirit" are synonymous with "wind". Nothing is more exciting than walking with the Spirit of God! Many times you do not even know where He will take you next, for walking in the Spirit is a life of spontaneity, discovery, and incomparable excitement and fulfillment! I dare you to tell God, "I will do anything You want, I will go anywhere You want, I will follow You wherever You lead me!" and pray that in all sincerity and faith. How God delights to answer such prayers of submission and surrender! No more excuses, obey. We would obey an earthly commanding officer; how much more are we to obey the Supreme Commander Who has enlisted us into His army (2 Timothy 2:3, 4)!

Father, You said that rebellion is as the sin of witchcraft. Forgive us for the ways in which we have thought obeying You was an "option." We want to show You the authenticity of our love for You by walking in obedience. Holy Spirit, forgive us for the times we have grieved You. In Your mercy, sensitize us again to Your still, small voice and let us follow wherever You carry us. We want to really know what it means to walk in the Spirit, Father. Thank You for hearing our prayer in Jesus Name.

CHAPTER 4

Elijah, a Man Dependent on God Even for Simple Necessities

The ravens brought him bread and meat in the morning, and bread and meat in the evening; and he drank from the brook.

1 Kings 17:6

What a powerful picture of Elijah's dependence on God (and of Psalm 23:1-2), and how perfectly it connects with how Jesus taught us to pray, "Give us today our daily bread." This was what God showed the Israelites in the wilderness through the manna. If they tried to store the manna it would rot. If they were putting their confidence in themselves to save themselves it would fail. God wanted them to know "whoever trusts in the LORD shall be safe" (Proverbs 29:25).

Beware of putting your trust in riches and in your bank account! As fast as money comes, it can leave even faster. "Do not overwork to be rich; because of your own understanding, cease! Will you set your eyes on that which is not? For riches certainly make themselves wings; they fly away like an eagle toward heaven" (Proverbs 23:4-5). Your dependence—for everything —must be in God alone.

We are the Body of Christ. Whatever we have been given is a blessing from God. He wants you, as part of the Body of Christ, to completely depend on Him, and He wants to use you as His instrument, as His channel to meet the needs of someone else. This was the model of the early church. They shared together so that no one had need or was found wanting (Acts 4:34).

Jesus spoke of a man who built bigger barns in which to store his riches so that he could then "take it easy." It sounds as if this man were more preoccupied about his retirement than he was about investing in the things of God. God's response to this is, "Fool! This night your soul will be required of you; then whose will those things be which you have provided?"

Jesus gives the application of the parable in the next verse, "So is he who lays up treasure for himself, and is not rich toward God" (Luke 12:20-21).

Interestingly, the man did not discern the blessing of God and what to do with it. It was not to be just for himself so that he could sit on his riches, but be used for the glory of God. Money is to be used for the advancement of the Kingdom of God and to help the poor in their distress. We are not to store our treasures on earth but to store them in heaven! Jesus is clear: "Seek first the Kingdom of God and His righteousness, and all these things shall be added to you" (Matthew 6:33). Put your faith in God, not in your work, not your bank account, and not in your investments. There is no true security outside of God's security. "If riches increase, do not set your heart on them" (Psalm 62:10b).

Heed the words of Jesus, "But take heed to yourselves, lest your hearts be weighed down with carousing, drunkenness, and cares of this life, and that Day come on you unexpectedly. For it will come as a snare on all those who dwell on the face of the whole earth. Watch therefore, and pray always that you may be counted worthy to escape all these things that will come to pass, and to stand before the Son of Man" (Luke 21:34-36).

Being constantly in prayer puts us in a position of dependence, even in the simple necessities. It is not taking anything for granted but to giving glory to God in everything. It is to be living simply, with gratitude, as the early church modeled for us.

"So continuing daily with one accord in the temple, and breaking bread from house to house, they ate their food with gladness and simplicity of heart, praising God and having favor with all the people. And the Lord added to the church daily those who were being saved" (Acts 2:46-47).

It was God who gave Job his wealth, and today, as then, God is the One who can take it away.

Let us trust in God for our daily bread, He is faithful to provide.

When I was in Tanzania, East Africa, our team traveled over to the island of Zanzibar for a few days. One morning while in prayer, I saw the Scripture reference "Proverbs 10:3" flash through my mind. Turning to it, I saw the promise of God, "The LORD will not permit the righteous to go hungry." It did not make sense in that moment why God would speak that to me. A few hours later, our team leaders called us together for a meeting. They said that they had discovered that a large amount of our team's money was stolen, and they told us that we did not have enough to buy food for everyone, that we were going to have to fast. There was just a little money left that could be used for food, and they were going to go into the city Zanzibar Town to see what little they could buy. One of the team leaders asked me to come with her. As we went into Zanzibar Town, I realized that we were in a vulnerable position because we did not speak the language and we were obviously foreigners. How easy it would be for people to take advantage of us. Suddenly a boy, I would say about the age of nine or ten, came up to us out of nowhere in the busy street. He told us (in clear English!) that his name was "Safe"—I kid you not—and that we should give him the money we had so that he could go and buy food for us. This boy then took what little we had (why would he suddenly come asking for our money so he could help us without prior knowledge of our situation anyway?) and went into the market. Some minutes later he returned with a lot of food! More than we could ever have bought! There was some money left over, and when our team leader offered to give him money, he refused. Then he walked out into the busy street until out of sight. It was soon after that I remembered what God told me that very morning in Proverbs 10:3! God is faithful, and He will supply all our **need** according to His riches in glory (Philippians 4:19, emphasis mine).

I remember a time in our first year of marriage, where Katie and I faced financial difficulty. She was pregnant with Abigail and bed ridden for most of her nine months of pregnancy because of her condition with hyperemesis gravidarum. She made a list of food to buy for the store that would hold us over for the week. Not wanting to alarm her because of our financial situation, I said nothing. I took the list wondering how God was going to answer and provide for us. I made way for the campus post office first, and found a slip of paper in our box, notifying we had a package. When I gave the slip of paper to the post office worker, she returned with two grocery bags full of food, which had been given anonymously. You probably guessed it, everything on the list Katie made for me was there, and much more. How true are the words of Jesus, "Of how much greater value or you…" in Matthew 6. Brother, He has eye on the sparrow, and truly He has His eye on you and I. He knows what we need before we ask. May we truly see our dependence on Him, and say with Paul whether we live in plenty or in want, we can do all through Christ Who strengthens us.

Father, open our eyes to see the absolute dependence we have upon You—for everything! Forgive us for our pride, our self-dependence, our prayerlessness, and our thanklessness. Today we declare that every good and perfect gift comes from You, and therefore all glory, praise, and thanks goes to You. Father, let us not only be thankful for Your meeting our needs according to Your riches and glory, but let us be channels of Your blessing to meet the needs of others. Please help us to see where the need is, that we may come and minister to that need in Jesus Name.

CHAPTER 5

Elijah, a Man Who Waited on the Lord for Direction

And it happened after a while that the brook dried up, because there had been no rain in the land. Then the word of the LORD came to him, saying, 'Arise, go to Zarephath, which belongs to Sidon, and dwell there. See, I have commanded a widow there to provide for you.'

1 Kings 17:7-9

Notice here you do not see Elijah flipping out and saying "What now!?!" or "Why have you forsaken me, God, and left me here to starve to death or to die of thirst?" He was watching as that brook was slowly drying up, but there is no indication that he felt he needed to inform God of his situation with a voice of panic. He knew God was in control. He knew he was in the will of God. He would wait on the Lord with trust and faith.

This was a difference in the lives of David and Saul and another reason why one, David, was successful and the other, Saul, saw defeat. Saul was presumptuous and took matters into his own hands (1 Samuel 13:8-12), whereas David waited to receive direction from God (1 Samuel 23:2).

It is in waiting on God that demonstrates faith. It also shows dependence on God for His guidance and counsel.

A friend of mine who met Richard Wurmbrand, the faithful servant of God who started "Voices of the Martyrs," told me of Wurmbrand's response when he was asked for his advice on the strategy for missions. Mr. Wurmbrand simply responded, "To wait on the Lord." My friend said you could sense the disappointment from the many waiting for some incredible unthought-of revelation from heaven. They did not get it.

What a dreadful thing it would be to realize that, rather than doing God's work and asking Him to bless it, you have been laboring on your own and have been asking God to bless your work, even though He never led you to do it. What a dreadful thing to see little fruit (that remains) after years of ministry and have little assurance that the Spirit was leading you. It is time, Brother, to stop the daily machinery and ask, "Is God in this?" and if He is not, to stop! The most precious commodity we have is time, and we are called to redeem it, not to waste it (Ephesians 5:15-17). We are not to be foolish but to understand what God's will is! Do not be foolish. Wait on God; ask Him to reveal what is of Him and what is not. Let us not stop there, but let us pray the apostolic prayer, "And this I pray, that your love may abound still more and more in knowledge and all discernment, that you may approve the things that are excellent, that you may be sincere and without offense till the day of Christ" (Philippians 1:9-10, emphasis mine).

In other words, we can settle for good things or ask God to reveal to us by His Spirit what is excellent. We have one life to live, one shot at this; let us make the most of it as we wait on God for His direction and His counsel. In so doing we will not be fretful or anxious, but truly His peace will guard our hearts and minds in Christ Jesus (Philippians 4:6-7). We will be walking by faith and not by sight (2 Corinthians 5:7), and we will fulfill the command of God in Colossians 3:15 that we let His peace rule in our hearts knowing He is truly leading our lives.

What is God's promise to us? "I will instruct you and teach you in the way you should go; I will guide you with My eye" (Psalm 32:8). And what is our responsibility? "Do not be like the horse or like the mule, which have no understanding, which must be harnessed with bit and bridle" (Psalm 32:9).

In other words, do not jump ahead as the horse (and not wait for the prompting of Your Lord) and do not lag behind in stubbornness as the mule! As you wait on the Lord, you will see a difference in your attitude. You will not be as easily angered or frustrated. You will not be as quick to seek your own remedy. You will sense your strength being renewed. You will be not be inclined to get back at someone, but rather will entrust him or her into the hands of God. You will find hope rise in your heart in the darkest of situations, and God has called you to be an agent of hope, as we will see in the next chapter.

When I received the calling of God to go and preach His Gospel overseas, I was ready to go right away! However, I was told by my mentor to go to a Bible college (he specifically felt God speak to him about Moody Bible Institute). I thought "Bible College? I'm ready to go now! I don't want to wait four more years!" As I prayed, God began to put on my heart the possibility of Bible College, but I still did not feel complete peace. As we wait on God, He is so faithful to send confirmation (2 Corinthians 13:1). Soon I was introduced to a graduate of Moody who had moved to my hometown (in fact he was the first black student body president of Moody and a man of God who has planted a large church in Maryland).

I continued to wait in prayer for another confirmation. One day at work, as I was helping to close up, a lady would not let me go, but asked me specifically to help her carry her purchases to her car. As I took her things to the car, I noticed she was from another State. I soon found out that she was a believer, and as she kept talking, she suddenly turned to me and said, "So you're going to Moody? (Remember, I had not even been accepted yet) That's great. A lot of schools have turned to liberal theology, not rightly interpreting the Word of God, but Moody is still holding to the conservative teaching of the Word." And with that, this woman, who I never met or saw again, delivered the message from God and drove off. I look back to that day now, as I am directing a discipleship school that covers all areas of theology and is training indigenous pastors and missionaries, and I know that the education I received at Moody has enabled me to do what I am doing and to create a curriculum that rightly handles the Word of God (2 Timothy 2:15). God knows what is best; we must be careful to wait on Him for confirmation and counsel. Whether they be big life decisions or seemingly much smaller daily dilemmas. He's waiting to direct us, if we would but ask and look for His counsel.

I encourage you to read the following verses out loud, praying the truths of them in your life in Jesus Name:

"Lead me in Your truth and teach me, for You are the God of my salvation; on You I wait all the day" (Psalm 25:5).

"Wait on the LORD; be of good courage, and He shall strengthen your heart; wait, I say, on the LORD!" (Psalm 27:14)!

"Rest in the LORD, and wait patiently for Him; do not fret because of him who prospers in his way, because of the man who brings wicked schemes to pass. Cease from anger, and forsake wrath; do not fret—it only causes harm. For evildoers shall be cut off; but those who wait on the LORD, they shall inherit the earth" (Psalm 37:7-9).

"Wait on the LORD, and keep His way, and He shall exalt you to inherit the land; when the wicked are cut off, you shall see it" (Psalm 37:34).

"I will wait for You, O You his Strength; for God is my defense" (Psalm 59:9).

"My soul, wait silently for God alone, for my expectation is from Him" (Psalm 62:5).

"Behold, as the eyes of servants look to the hand of their masters, as the eyes of a maid to the hand of her mistress, so our eyes look to the LORD our God, until he has mercy on us" (Psalm 123:2).

"I wait for the LORD, my soul waits, and in His word I do hope" (Psalm 130:5).

"Do not say, 'I will recompense evil'; wait for the Lord, and He will save you" (Proverbs 20:22).

"Therefore the LORD will wait, that He may be gracious to you; and therefore He will be exalted, that He may have mercy on you. For the LORD is a God of justice; blessed are all those who wait for Him" (Isaiah 30:18).

"But those who wait on the LORD shall renew their strength;

they shall mount up with wings like eagles, they shall run and not be weary, they shall walk and not faint" (Isaiah 40:31).

"So you, by the help of your God, return; observe mercy and justice, and wait on your God continually" (Hosea 12:6).

"Therefore I will look to the LORD; I will wait for the God of my salvation; my God will hear me" (Micah 7:7).

CHAPTER 6

Elijah, a Man Who Brought Hope to the Hopeless

So she said, "As the LORD your God lives, I do not have bread, only a handful of flour in a bin, and a little oil in a jar; and see, I am gathering a couple of sticks that I may go in and prepare it for myself and my son, that we may eat it, and die." And Elijah said to her, 'Do not fear; go and do as you have said, but make me a small cake from it first, and bring it to me; and afterward make some for yourself and your son. For thus says the LORD God of Israel: "The bin of flour shall not be used up, nor shall the jar of oil run dry, until the day the LORD sends rain on the earth."'

1 Kings 17:12-14

Where Jesus is, there is life. He is the bread of life, and He is the living water. He promises to those that would believe in Him that out of their hearts would flow rivers of living water (John 7:37-39). Jesus makes possibilities where there are impossibilities. We too are to bring such life, such hope as His ambassadors. The atmosphere should change wherever we are, simply because Jesus is with us! Darkness brings depression and despair, but light brings revelation, vision, perspective, and hope.

I went to high school with a guy who had so many gifts and so many things going for him, yet he later committed suicide by putting a knife into his chest. How many are living in hopelessness, despair, and deep depression? According to statistics, more than ever. The suicide rate continues to climb. So many are in pain as a result of curses spoken over them by their parents or peers. So many are overwhelmed with the problems of life, coming to the end of their rope and seeing no way out. O, men of God, it is time to be used of God, led of His Spirit to bring such people hope and to let them know there is an answer! There is Someone Who loves them, Who proves His love for them in that while they are still sinners, He died for them! There IS light at the end of the tunnel!

How often it is the depressed and dejected that are searching, whose hearts are open to receive the truth. It also can just as easily be the ones who "have it all" and appear to scoff at the idea of needing God, who God continues to send to you because they too are in need of hope. Keep in mind that those who think they "have it all" can be of any economic status, just as those who are filled with despair, pain and hopelessness can be of any economic status.

I have a friend whom God uses to minister to the richest of the rich, but he testifies that many of them are filled with depression and hopelessness and are searching because they realize that money has not and does not answer the bigger "life questions" or bring them a sense of significance. This friend leads them to know and understand the higher purpose in life and the truth that "it is more blessed to give than to receive."

Some people are able to cover their pain extremely well. This is why we must never judge according to appearances, but be led by the Holy Spirit (Isaiah 11:2-4). So often different types of addictions are really symptoms of a greater heart need. It could be drugs or alcohol or whatever, they are ways the individual has sought to mask the hopelessness and pain inside.

Over the years I have been amazed at just how widespread depression and hopelessness is, and how well people hide it. It could be someone that appears "successful" to the world, or it could be someone that has been written off by society. Many that have been institutionalized and heavily medicated really just need the light of God's hope and love to bring inner healing in their spirits. I have personally seen God deliver those that were labeled as insane and out of their minds, healed by the power of the Holy Spirit. I'm talking about those that were given a sound mind, and testified they felt their minds come back together. We are not just body, but body, spirit and soul and each of these three can affect the other very quickly and very easily. The body can be medicated but if the spirit is broken and "bleeding" it will just be a band-aid on a gaping wound. In dealing with the spirit, they may just find the other physical symptoms leaving. A little love will go a long way. Next time you're tempted to judge, ask God for revelation, He is able to show you the greater need. Perhaps it will make more sense when you see the greater picture, the full story.

May we be spiritually alert when someone is gripped in depression and despair. Sometimes all it takes is a physical touch to show a person that someone cares. This simple act can become an open door for them through which they may pour out their pain—for we know there is healing through confession (James 5:16). That person you meet who "flies of the handle" in anger may be doing that because of deep pain. Be careful how you respond.

It is time to be used of God to reveal to others the Kingdom of God, a kingdom of hope that does not focus on the things of this world (which is passing away with all its lusts) but on the One to come (Colossians 3:1-2). Sin keeps us focused on ourselves, but when we walk with God in holiness and freedom we focus on serving others. Our desire becomes to spend our time ministering to others and not to be self-absorbed.

The Spirit of the Lord was upon Jesus and anointed Him to preach good news to the poor, to heal the broken hearted, to preach deliverance to the captives and recovery of sight to the blind, to set at liberty those who are oppressed, and to preach the acceptable year of the Lord (Luke 4:18). That same Spirit of God is upon us! How many are searching for a way out. When we are abandoned to God, walking in His will, He can send us and lead us to minister to the hopeless, so that they can know the way, the truth, and the life, our Lord Jesus Christ!

O God send us out to be Your instruments of hope and life, and to be a light in the darkness, pointing them to You. Save, deliver, and heal today Father in Jesus Name we pray! Send the truly depressed and despairing to us and let us proclaim healing to their broken hearts, and freedom from their oppression. Sensitize us Holy Spirit to see those who need Your hope, and give us the courage to not only speak Your love, but demonstrate it.

Week #1
Discussion questions and points of application

1. Have you surrendered everything to your Lord Jesus? Remember if we are a part of the Kingdom of God, everything in our lives is to be submitted to the King. Set a time aside to declare the Lordship of Jesus over every area of your heart, over your family and in your home. It's really to be His heart, His home and His family, Amen? Ask the Holy Spirit to walk you through your home to see if there is anything that is grieving Him. Ask Him to your fill life, heart and home with His glory as you clean "house."

2. As has been pointed out, you know you are free when you can use what the enemy sought to destroy you with, to testify of what you have been delivered from and get others freed from that same former bondage. How can God use previous bondage in your life to bring a message of hope to those around you? Share your testimony of what God has delivered you from with brothers in Christ and let it edify and encourage.

3. What practical steps can you take to establish a family altar?

4. Some memorize more through audio, others visual, still others kinetically, what way do you find best for you? What practical steps will you take to memorize the Word of God starting today? What practical ways can we be like

Joshua and David and meditate on the Word continually? What does boldness look like to you? Pray for boldness together for each other.

5. Give a testimony of when you acted in obedience and saw God at work. What are the signs of when you know you are walking in disobedience?

6. Give a testimony of either (1) how God provided for you in time of need (2) God may have led you to help someone in need and the joy it brought or (3) what things help remind you of God's abundant provision in your life and brings thanksgiving from your heart to God. Ask God to use you to be a channel of His provision to someone in need.

7. If you have had a time of great depression in your life, share how you expressed that depression, and what was used to bring you out of it. Pray and ask God to reveal anyone in your life now that is battling hopelessness and depression and then bring a letter, prayer or word of encouragement.

CHAPTER 7

Elijah, a Man Who Brought a Prophet's Reward to Those Who Received Him

So she went away and did according to the word of Elijah; and she and he and her household ate for many days. The bin of flour was not used up, nor did the jar of oil run dry, according to the word of the LORD which He spoke by Elijah.
1 Kings 17:15-16

Not only should we bring hope, we should bring the blessing of God. Those around us should see the favor of God on our lives and will want to walk as we walk with God. Such was the testimony of men of God like Abraham, Joseph, Moses, Samuel, and Daniel in the Old Testament. The Word reveals that one can grow in favor with both God and man (Luke 2:52) and in "His favor is for life" (Psalm 30:15). We can ask for God's favor (Psalm 119:58), but we must remember that it is not divorced from the fruit of a life that walks with God (Proverbs 12:2, 14:9).

The words of Jesus should bear truth in our lives, "He who receives a prophet in the name of a prophet shall receive a prophet's reward. And he who receives a righteous man in the name of a righteous man shall receive a righteous man's reward" (Matthew 10:41). The context of this verse is, of course, crucial. The context was Jesus' commissioning the disciples to go preach the Gospel of the Kingdom. It was in walking in the will of God, being about the King's business, that such a promise was given. Jesus says it is the pagans that are consumed and concerned with eating, clothes, and the things of this world. The Father knows what we need! However, God can use the blessing of the prophet to reveal to the unbeliever's eyes that God is with him!

I remember that at the time I married Katie I had been doing temporary work in Maryland. We would only be living in Maryland for about five months before moving to Chicago. On our flight to Florida for our honeymoon, I turned to the man who was sitting next to me, striking up a conversation and looking for an opportunity to tell him the Good News. As I was sharing, he suddenly asked me if I wanted a job, even though I had not mentioned my needing one. It turned out that this man was the co-owner of one of the most respected wood flooring companies in Maryland as well as the bordering counties in Pennsylvania and Virginia. He offered me, on the spot, an incredible starting position and good pay for those five months, and he was not even a believer! And why did he so quickly make me this offer? It was because he had previously hired a woman who was looking to become a missionary, and he was so impressed with her work ethic and the blessing of God on her life that he told himself if he came across anyone else looking to become a missionary, he would hire him/her on the spot! During our conversation I had shared I was going to Moody Bible Institute to become a missionary. He had seen the righteous person's reward. He had seen the favor of God on the woman's life he had hired and it had opened his eyes and ears to wanting to hear more of Jesus.

Let us model a life that is Kingdom-focused, and we will draw the attention of the world to see that God is with us, but it will not be for us to preach to them "The Seven Secrets of Successful Living!" It will be for us to point them to Jesus! To make them ready for the King of Glory! It will be for us to help them not focus on the reward and the blessing, but the Giver of the reward and the Source of the blessing! O God, forgive us for corrupting Your message. So many in the Church are focusing on things that are temporary and not on things that are eternal! May we be used to bring Your blessing and favor like Joseph, for the saving of lives! Father help us see that when we are promoted it is not for the sake of the promotion, but for us to be in a greater position to be a "Joseph" for the saving of many lives and for the preparation of others for the Day of the Lord's coming! In Jesus' Name!

CHAPTER 8

Elijah, a Man Whose Very Presence Brought Conviction by the Spirit

Now it happened after these things that the son of the woman who owned the house became sick. And his sickness was so serious that there was no breath left in him. So she said to Elijah, What have I to do with you, O man of God? Have you come to me to bring my sin to remembrance, and to kill my son?

1 Kings 17:17-18

The testimony of men of God like Smith Wigglesworth and Charles Finney is that they would convict men of sin even when they had not said a word. They were carriers of the presence of God; the Light in them shown so brightly in the spirit world that even the natural world felt it and reacted to it. Brother, do not be satisfied that this degree of sanctification was for them and not for you. Our motivation is not to bring attention to ourselves as some kind of "spiritual giant," but to bring the Kingdom, to bring a consciousness of God. His presence should lead to a point of decision! As Leonard Ravenhill said in regards to how too often the Church wants to be accepted by the world, to be so relevant (and therefore many times so compromised), "How is it the world couldn't get on with the holiest Man that ever lived and can get on with you and me? Are we compromised? Have we no spiritual stature? Have we no righteousness that reflects on their corruption?"

When Jesus walked the earth, there was an immediate reaction to His presence, either one of attraction or repulsion. The demons could not keep quiet or hide in His presence. And now Jesus says in John 20:21, "As the Father has sent Me, I also send you." As we walk in the light as He in the light, we will illuminate the very spiritual atmosphere, wherever we are. This is not a Pharisaical judgmental disposition. This is not a self-righteous attitude that looks down on others, but a true holiness that brings the revelation of God's true character, that they might turn to God and be saved, be delivered, and be healed. God commands us to "have no fellowship with the unfruitful works of darkness, but rather expose them" (Ephesians 5:11). Our lives should bring a clear revelation of the nature of Jesus. "He who says he abides in Him ought himself also to walk just as He walked" (1 John 2:6). Those around us should make no mistake; we are children of the Light! When others are around us, they should not be telling the same jokes because of God's presence in our lives. They should actually be careful of their words, they should "feel" God on our lives. If we are walking with God, we should find people actually apologizing for their behavior or words. This is the door God has opened for us, to tell them the truth in love and humility! We are not to say, "It's okay," because of a lack of boldness or to avoid having the appearance of some kind of pious, holier-than-thou attitude, but to share the Word of God and our testimony. (I speak this having experienced this. I began to notice people, who normally thought nothing of what they said, apologizing to me for their words. At first I did not take advantage of it, until the Lord rebuked me and showed me that this was His door). If we are truly in the Spirit, then the Spirit of God will work in and through us to convict the world of sin, righteousness, and the judgment to come (John 16:8). Moses prayed out, "If Your presence does not go with us, do not lead us up from here. For how then can it be known that I have found favor in Your sight, I and Your people? Is it not by Your going with us, so that we, I and Your people, may be distinguished from all the other people who are upon the face of the earth?"(Exodus 33:15-16, NASB, emphasis mine).

Father, fill us with Your Spirit we ask! Let us walk in the light as You are in the light. Let us be carriers of Your divine Presence! Let us be that city set on a hill that cannot be hid, the lamp that gives light to all in the house! Let our lives, our very presence; bear witness that You are with us! For if Your Presence is not with us, what will mark us as different from all the other people of the world? We want Your manifest Presence to fill our lives, Father! We love You! In the name of Jesus, be glorified in our lives!

CHAPTER 9

Elijah, a Man Full of the Mercy and Compassion of God

*And he said to her, "Give me your son." So he took
him out of her arms and carried him to the upper
room where he was staying and laid him on his
own bed. Then he cried out to the LORD and said,
"O LORD my God, have you also brought tragedy
on the widow with whom I lodge, by killing her
son?" And he stretched himself out on the child
three times, and cried out to the LORD and said,
"O LORD my God, I pray, let this child's soul
come back to him."*

1 Kings 17:19-21

Love enters into the situations, pains, and trials of others.
Love empathizes.

Empathy- (noun) – the ability to understand and share the

feelings of another. Origin early 20th century from Greek empatheia (em (in) pathos (feeling). (Definition taken from the New Oxford American Dictionary.)

It is one thing to "pray for someone;" it is another thing to enter into his or her pain and trial. It is one thing to pass by and listen and another thing to stop, stay and help. It is one thing to fulfill a religious duty; it is another thing to feel the burden, the sorrow, and the length and depth of someone's circumstance! When we pray we need to enter—to enter into their world, to enter into their pain, to enter into God's heart for them. This is true praying, it is not merely giving a look of sympathy, saying a few prayers, and moving on.

Jesus warned that it was because of sin that the love of many would grow cold (Matthew 24:12). Sin hardens you; sin makes you indifferent and apathetic. When we are walking in holiness, walking in His will, bringing hope to the hopeless, we are going to find ourselves increasingly where God's heart is, and we will share His heart. We will fulfill the Scripture, "Rejoice with those who rejoice and weep with those who weep" (Romans 12:15), and "bear one another's burdens, and so fulfill the law of Christ" (Galatians 6:2, emphasis mine).

We are going to take responsibility and be men of commitment. We will not walk away; we will have a "stick-to-it-iveness." We are going to pray for someone else in the same way we would want others to pray for us. We are going to walk with someone through the valley of the shadow of death just as we would want someone to be there with us. We are going to persevere with others in the same way we would want them to persevere with and for us and so fulfill the command of Jesus, "Therefore, whatever you want men to do to you, do also to them, for this is the Law and the Prophets" (Matthew 7:12).

Instead of retreating to our comfortable houses and being satisfied with our leisure time ("after all I deserve it, right?"), we are going to go where others live in their pain and wrestle with the issues with them and so experience the Scripture that tells us that "a brother is born for adversity" (Proverbs 17:17). If we are where the battle is, we will not forget what the battle is, for it will be before our eyes. However, if we surround ourselves with what is comfortable and live sheltered lives, we are living in a dream world and may get a rude awakening as the goats did, in Matthew 25:31-46, missing where Jesus was making Himself visible!

"In as much as you did not do it to one of the least of these..."

Remember where He said we would find Him? Not in the place many were looking. He was hungry, thirsty, a stranger, naked, sick, and in prison. These are places we also should seek Jesus revealing Himself today, that we may live in the compassion and manifestation of Christ-love, empathizing, loving not just in word but in action (1 John 3:18).

In order to empathize, you must—you *have* to—be pulled out of your comfort zone. You are going to be inconvenienced just as the Good Samaritan was (Luke 10:25-37). You are going to have to stop in the midst of your busy schedule, in the midst of your full calendar and be ready to make time to minister to those in need. You and I need to constantly be asking ourselves, "How can I be Jesus to this person in this moment? How would I want someone to respond to me if I was in this situation?" The flesh will immediately cry out and resist, but if you refuse to listen to it, and instead allow the Spirit to work, you will find it will be the highlight of your day—every time! Why? Because you have entered into the "good works, which God prepared beforehand that we should walk in them" (Ephesians 2:10).

Some of my fondest memories are centered around nights on the streets of Chicago ministering to the homeless with brothers in Christ. My schedule was already full with being a full time student and working, but I made time. It was during those times I witnessed some of the most amazing moments of the glory of God!

I remember being with two brothers ministering on the cold streets of Chicago one wintry night in the area of Lower Wacker Street. At that time, Lower Wacker was the center of the greatest homeless population in Chicago as well as significant gang activity. We began talking with a homeless man, and, as God allowed us to enter into his world and He filled us with His love for this man, we led him to the feet of Jesus, where he surrendered himself to the Lord. But that was not all; we were yet to see more of God's glory that night! For, as we were praying, a sharply dressed man, wearing clothes that were probably worth more than ALL the clothes I owned put together and wearing a lot of gold jewelry, walked up and bowed his head with us. He had been listening to our conversation with this homeless man. When we grabbed the hands of this homeless man (now our brother!) to form a circle, this well dressed man stepped in and grabbed our hands and also prayed out right there to give his life to Jesus. As we walked back to Moody Bible Institute together, we learned that his name was Joe. We also found out that he was a leader of a well-known gang. Joe told us he was turning from the gang life and was now going to follow Jesus. He was filled with the Spirit as he sang out a spontaneous song to the Lord!

When we arrived at Moody (it was now about eleven o'clock), we were exhorting him to keep walking with God. All of a sudden, I literally felt an evil presence coming from behind. A man suddenly appeared, concealing his hand in his coat, and began telling Joe and the three of us what he had come to do. He was a rival gang member. I could sense a spirit of death and murder on this man. I realized that if God willed it, this man could pull out the gun he was holding inside his coat and kill us. Instead, we watched as the power of God arrested this man. It was as if he tried several times to pull the gun out but could not! He cussed and yelled in rage, but He was stopped by the power of God.

Finally, he turned and left. Joe then spoke to us and in a voice that was as smooth and calm as any voice you have heard, asked us (these three young, white college men from suburban homes), "You weren't scared, were you?"

I admitted that it was a real test for me! Joe said, "That's how I live every day. I wake up every day realizing that it could be my last. I walk around every corner knowing that I could be killed."

Then, Joe spoke about the man who had walked away. "He broke gang rules. He came high on 'caine (cocaine). If you are going to kill a man, you don't do it with drugs. I almost made him a pumpkin head, but I'm not walking that road anymore. I'm walking with Jesus now." GLORY!

Joe himself now had entered into the love of God. As he left us late that night and I saw him disappearing into the dark, I will never forget God's answer to me in response to how concerned I was for his safety, wondering if that other man was waiting for him. God spoke to my heart, reassuring me that Joe belonged to Him now and that He was able to protect His own. Had I not taken time to enter into another's world, I would have missed seeing God's glory in Joe's life. As we enter into the needs of others rather than just pass by, we will see God's glory. Just as Elijah saw the resurrection of the woman's son, (like Joe, who was dead in his sins, entering into a new life in Christ).

Love is stronger than hatred and vengeance! Mercy triumphs over judgment! Compassion is contagious! HalleluYah! Enter into the heart of God's love, and you will find yourself in places and talking with people that you never could have imagined. And remember, "Perfect love casts out fear" (1 John 4:18).

Father, baptize our hearts with Your love, we pray, in Jesus' Name!

CHAPTER 10

Elijah, a Man Whose Message Was Validated by Miracles and Answered Prayer

Then LORD heard the voice of Elijah; and the soul of the child came back to him, and he revived. And Elijah took the child and brought him down from the upper room into the house, and gave him to his mother. And Elijah said, "See, your son lives!" Then the woman said to Elijah, "Now by this I know that you are a man of God, and that the word of the LORD in your mouth is the truth."

1 Kings 17:22-24

Jesus said, "If I do not do the works of My Father, do not believe Me; but if I do, though you do not believe Me, believe the works, that you may know and believe that the Father is in Me, and I in Him" (John 10:37-38).

As the old saying goes, "Your actions speak so loud, I can't hear what you're saying." So the acts of God speak of our great God! Paul says the Kingdom of God is not in word but in power (1 Corinthians 4:20)!

Why did he say this? Paul declared, "And my speech and my preaching were not with persuasive words of human wisdom, but in demonstration of the Spirit and of power, <u>that your faith</u> should not be in the wisdom of men but in the power of God" (1 Corinthians 2:4-5, emphasis mine).

A friend came to visit me in Guinea Bissau and brought a copy of <u>Christianity Today</u> in which there was an article called "The New Apostate." It described the alarming number of people leaving the church and walking away from the things of God they had grown up with. Some of them became agnostics or atheists; some tried other religions such as Wicca. As I prayed through it, I felt the Spirit reveal something that was not mentioned in the article: that there are many in the church whose faith is based strictly on knowledge, rather than being based on experience and the power of God. There is a saying that one who has a testimony is never at the hands of one who has merely an argument. As easily as someone is convinced by argument to follow, they can be convinced by an argument to leave. For too long many in the church have given their children a doctrinal list of do's and don'ts, but not an experience with God. Christianity void of power is not biblical! Yet we have created a theology in many of our seminaries and bible colleges that denies the power of God or tries to explain it away with a few discreet verses, while ignoring the overwhelming number of scriptures that say otherwise. We are reaping what we have sown,

Brothers! These schools have produced a group of pastors that have taken in the leaven of the Sadducees, denying the supernatural. How can anyone read the book of Acts and not see the connection that the Word is validated with power? As missionaries in West Africa, we would never have had the ear of some people if there were not a demonstration of the Spirit's power. Africans are pragmatic people; if I am not bringing the revelation of God's Kingdom in power over demons and disease, then why should they believe that Christianity is superior to Islam or to their witchdoctors? It was Jesus who said, "If I cast out demons by the Spirit of God, surely the kingdom of God has come upon you" (Matthew 12:28). As a Church, we need to repent of this spirit of unbelief, of always rationalizing the supernatural, of not believing Jesus when He declared He really is the same yesterday, today, and forever. And since Jesus is the same, He not only says the same things, He does the same things. Jesus came to reveal the will of the Father which was validated by miracles He then gave the promise that his followers would also experience the miraculous (John 14:9-14).

Perhaps you grew up, as I did, largely in circles that deny that the spiritual gifts are for today. Perhaps you are in such a circle now. You have a choice. You could deny the clear example of Scripture, deny the testimonies of tens of thousands around the world who have seen or are seeing the power of God on a regular basis, and call your brothers in charismatic circles liars and deceived, or you can humble yourself, ask God to show you His power, and have a teachable attitude (even if you have had a bad experience in the past with a charismatic brother or church. Please stop "throwing out the baby with the bathwater.")

How easy it is to surround oneself in a certain circles of theology, teaching and friends, and believe that it represents all there is to Christianity and that such miracles do not happen today. It is amazing that someone can go through life being fully convinced of this, and yet right in his own city there could be a group of people experiencing the miraculous on a regular basis—if only his eyes were opened to see.

The promise—to *find*—is given to those who *seek* (Matthew 7:7).

For the longest time, I did not see the miraculous, but I knew that there must be more, simply by the witness of the Spirit and the Word of God. God is faithful; He will honor the searching heart. Today I can personally testify to seeing many, many amazing miracles in my life to the glory of God. I have seen the lame walk, like the time a man who had suffered a stroke and needed a crutch to walk as the left side of his body was almost useless. As he experienced the power of God going through his body, full strength came to both his arm and leg. He was then was able to walk perfectly again and declared with a shout, "This cane is going into retirement!"

I can testify of a man instantly regaining the use of his arm. I have seen God give immediate relief from pain, as in the case of a woman whose arm had been in brace for years due to arthritic pain. She left our time of prayer instantly healed. At the same meeting there were others who had not been able to bend over or walk without pain who began to dance and exclaim, "God is in this place!"

I witnessed the healing of a woman who was diagnosed with cancer. She had to be catheterized, she was bent over in pain, and only a small percentage of her liver was functioning. Her doctors were telling her that the condition was only getting worse. As I was praying for her, she wept and cried out, "All the pain is gone!"

Then, weeping, she stood to her feet with arms raised! Later, she called to verify that the healing was real.

I have seen God restore hearing to a deaf ear.

I was privileged to see God use a brother in Christ, Joel Crumpton, to heal a man's eyes. This man was nearly blind from a chemical accident. Right before my own eyes I witnessed (and about twelve other men with us) this man's eyes actually change color, from a light gray to his natural dark brown—instantly! God gave him new eyes! Jesus is a healer! HalleluYah! He *is* the same yesterday, today, and forever (Hebrews 13:8).

For a period of time, I recorded personal testimonies of miracles of God's healing power that totaled about 80 typed pages of documentation. I recorded one after another, and I have only since stopped because of time (but continue to send out testimonies through emails and newsletters). I will say again to anyone who reads these testimonies and refuses to believe that God does these things today, you either have to call me a liar or re-examine your theology. If you have a heart for truth, you will search and find out if these things are so. I would be happy to forward that documentation to anyone wanting it (and to put you in contact with people such as Joel, who sees the miraculous on a weekly—sometimes daily—basis.)

God is no respecter of persons. He is looking to show Himself strong on behalf of those whose hearts are fully given to Him (2 Chronicles 16:9).

For me personally, this breakthrough came during a time of my seeking God's face on this matter, of renewing my mind in the truth of His Word, not in a man's theology that tries to explain away the miraculous. Faith comes by hearing the Word of God (Romans 10:17). It also helps to be around brothers who are walking in the power of God. Faith is contagious. Get around faith and the supernatural long enough and it will start to rub off on you. As Smith Wigglesworth used to say, "Only believe." All things are possible to them who believe. So believe, Brother, and stop *dis*believing (John 20:27). God wants to use you to validate His Kingdom through His power, not just in word. The command of God is that we should "earnestly desire the gifts" (1 Corinthians 12:31, 14:1). That is a command. I feel convicted to also write what the Spirit revealed to me after a long period of fasting and prayer. I was crying out for a long period of time (weeks and then months) for the "power" to see the miracles, to walk in the anointing. I finally heard the Spirit of God say to me, "The anointing will come when you love." As I've asked the Spirit to baptize me with His love, I have seen so much more of His power and anointing. We read many times before Jesus performed a miracle (whether the multiplication of the loaves and fishes or a healing) He was "moved with compassion." **The anointing operates out of a heart of love.**

We must address the need to avoid two extremes, one of which says that the Holy Spirit does not do these things today. Be careful if that is you. The context for quenching the Spirit of God in 1 Thessalonians 5 is "Do not despise prophecies." We are commanded, "Do not forbid to speak with tongues" (1 Corinthians 14:39). Who are you, O man, to tell God what He does and does not do, if He has revealed it in His eternal Word, specifically, in the Church age? He is God! Do you have no fear of God when telling the Holy Spirit that He does not do these things today? Can you be so bold as to make such a statement? Are you going to call hundreds of thousands and even millions (remember most of the Church is outside America) of other disciples of Christ "liars" who have personal testimonies of His gifts being exercised on a regular basis? (For just one powerful testimony of what God is doing overseas, read The Heavenly Man by Brother Yun). Are you prepared to stand before God on the Day of Judgment with absolute conviction and without a hint of doubt and make such a statement? If not, then who are you to be teaching others this same doctrine?

Jesus says, "Whoever therefore breaks one of these least of these commandments, and teaches men so, shall be called least in the kingdom of heaven; but whoever does and teaches them, he shall be called great in the kingdom of heaven" (Matthew 5:19).

Some in this camp think that they can choose which gifts of the Holy Spirit will be used and which will not, which gifts will be received and which ones will be rejected. Are we in a place to negotiate with Almighty God? Are we in a place to tell the Holy Spirit what He can and cannot do in our midst?

The other extreme is to treat the Holy Spirit as if He is a mere vending machine. Just push the right button and you will get something. Just do this formula and you, too, can start speaking in tongues; or you, too, can prophesy; or you, too, can do whatever you want.

The Holy Spirit is holy! How can so many forget 1 Corinthians 12:11? "But one and the same Spirit works all these things, distributing each one individually as He wills."

God made it clear in the Old Testament that those who did not reverence that which was holy were to be cut off. Remember the story of Aaron's sons (Leviticus 10) or of Uzzah when he improperly laid his hand upon the ark of God while it was being transported to Jerusalem (2 Samuel 6)? Remember how Moses was punished for not sanctifying the name of the Lord when he struck the rock twice (Numbers 20)?

Is He not the same God? Yet many treat the Holy Spirit as

if He were not the third person of the Godhead. Many seem to expect the Holy Spirit to do whatever they desire and when they desire it. Be careful! You are on dangerous ground. I speak that by the authority of the Scriptures. Just because one is not struck dead instantly for lying against the Holy Spirit, as Ananias and Sapphira were(Acts 5:1-10), that doesn't mean that God is not still the same, and that He is not still to be reverenced, and that He will not discipline. Jesus said He could do nothing of Himself but whatever He saw the Father doing He did likewise (John 5:19), we follow His leading, not tell Him what He needs to do for us.

Pastor David Yonggi Cho, pastor of the world's largest church, located in South Korea, gives a testimony in his <u>Lessons on Prayer</u>, "Tabernacle Prayer Course," which can be viewed online. Pastor Cho relates that when his church had reached 3,000 members, he was seeing no further growth. When he felt that he had tried everything he knew to do, he finally came to the end of himself. He prayed and prayed and asked God if that was as far as his church would grow. He shares that after he cried out to the Lord, he fell into a deep sleep and felt himself in the presence of God. Suddenly, the Father asked him if he wanted to see the church grow, to which Cho responded, "Yes, Father."

God asked him, "When the Israelites were in the wilderness, what would have happened if they had sought (to catch) the quail with their bare hands?"

Cho answered, "They would have probably had a lot of sunstroke."

God showed him it was the wind that brought the quail. God told Pastor Cho that he was trying to win souls in his own strength, but if he would depend on the Holy Spirit, He would bring the souls to Himself. Cho's response was that he *had* the Holy Spirit, that he'd been already baptized in the Holy Spirit, that he even speaks in tongues. Cho said to God, "I have all I need."

Then, Cho said the awesome voice of God, in strength and with sternness, spoke to him, "That's your trouble! You are treating the Holy Spirit impersonally, like an acrobat. He is a Holy Person! You need to surrender to the Holy Spirit. He needs to be your Senior Partner, the Senior Pastor! You are trying to *use* the Holy Spirit!"

Cho said he felt the fear of God and repented right there. He asked the Holy Spirit's forgiveness for treating him like an "acrobat." He immediately went to the Scripture passage, 2 Corinthians 13:14, and made it his personal meditation on the meaning of having communion with the Holy Spirit. He told the Holy Spirit, "If I would have treated my wife as I have treated You, my wife would have packed up and left a long time ago!"

Cho emphasizes—the Holy Spirit is a Person! He said that from that moment on he received and accepted that the Holy Spirit was to be the Senior Pastor. He would do nothing without the permission of the Holy Spirit.

Pastor Cho said that the church suddenly went from the 3,000 to 7,000 to 10,000 until it grew to be some 750,000 people!

Forgive us, Holy Spirit, for not depending on You and for not looking to bring the Kingdom of God in power. Forgive us for the unbelief in your Church. Forgive us for the way You have been addressed and for the way your Church has treated as common that which is holy. Teach us what it really means to have communion with You, Holy Spirit. Lord, use us as Your channels of power, that would point people to You, the living God. We earnestly desire spiritual gifts to see Your Kingdom come in power, and peoples faith to not rest in our wisdom but Your power. Restore us to Your standard, we ask, in Jesus' Name!

CHAPTER 11

Elijah, a Man of His Word

"And it shall come to pass, as soon as I am gone from you, that the Spirit of the LORD will carry you to a place I do not know; so when I go and tell Ahab, and he cannot find you, he will kill me. But I your servant have feared the LORD from my youth. Was it not reported to my lord what I did when Jezebel killed the prophets of the LORD, how I hid one hundred men of the LORD'S prophets, fifty to a cave, and fed them with bread and water? And now you say, 'Go, tell your master, "Elijah is here."' He will kill me!" Then Elijah said, "As the LORD of hosts lives, before whom I stand, I will surely present myself to him today."

1 Kings 18:12-15

A friend of mine received a revelation concerning the importance of being a person of one's word. He went to a Charismatic church where they talked about and preached the power of God but bore so few testimonies. He asked them to pray for him about a serious need in his life. When he followed up with this church, he realized that although they had heartily agreed to pray for him, they did not follow through with their commitment. He then went to another mainline denominational church that such a Charismatic church may jeer at as having no idea about the power of God. When my friend came to them with his requests, they not only said that they would pray, but they did pray—faithfully. He soon realized that they had testimonies of all kinds of answered prayer. This included his own prayer requests being powerfully answered by God. The Spirit quickly helped him to see the connection between spiritual authority, answered prayer, and being a person of one's word. He began to see more clearly that those who saw answered prayer on a regular basis were the same ones who were men of their word, men of covenant, and men of integrity.

One of the trespasses God lists in Leviticus 6 is swearing falsely (or not fulfilling a vow), which is also mentioned in Numbers 30:2. In God's eyes, saying that we will do something but failing to do it is a trespass. Jesus commands us not to give an oath, but to let our "yes be yes" and your "no be no" (Matthew 5:37). He says that anything more than this is of the evil one. Isn't it interesting that James gives the exact same warning in James 5 verse 12 but states that we are to have our "yes be yes" and "no be no" lest we fall into judgment. Look at the connection… the enemy knows that if he can tempt us in this area it will bring judgment. It's that serious to God and it is really a strategy of the devil.

Brother, it is time to repent of any and all times you have not fulfilled your word. This would include times you said you would "never" do that again, yet you have done it again or any other rash vow that you have broken. This includes financial obligations that you have not kept (and since forsaken) or times you told your family, a friend, or perhaps someone in the work place that you would do something and then did not. God takes our words seriously — every single one in fact (Matthew 12:36-37). The men God desires to see are men of integrity, men who will have the testimony of Samuel, "So Samuel grew, and the LORD was with him and let none of his words fall to the ground" (1 Samuel 3:19).

Most of this generation's words are of little value. God wants men who will pray with David, "Set a guard, O LORD, over my mouth; keep watch over the door of my lips" (Psalm 141:3).

Remember who God said would abide in His tabernacle and dwell in His holy hill? Of the many attributes listed, including those actually concerning the tongue, a specific one mentioned in Psalm 15 concerns the one "who swears to his own hurt and does not change." Such a one will "never be moved."

Reflect again and pray these Proverbs into your life:

10:19 "In the multitude of words sin is not lacking, but he who restrains his lips is wise."

11:3 "The integrity of the upright will guide them, but the perversity of the unfaithful will destroy them."

13:3 "He who guards his mouth preserves his life, but he who opens wide his lips shall have destruction."

15:28 "The heart of the righteous studies how to answer, but the mouth of the wicked pours forth evil."

19:1 "Better is the poor that walks in his integrity than one who is perverse in his lips, and is a fool."

20:7 "The righteous man walks in his integrity; his children are blessed after him."

21:23 "Whoever guards his mouth and tongue keeps his soul from troubles."

29:20 "Do you see a man hasty in his words? There is more hope for a fool than for him."

Brother, if you have broken your word, whether to God, to your wife, to your children, or in your work or among others, repent today. Repent, and be reminded that one day we will be held accountable for our words. It is a new day from this day forward. You are going to be a man of your word.

May we have the testimony of Job before our great Father, "Then the LORD said to Satan, 'Have you considered my servant Job, that there is none like him in the earth, a blameless and upright man, one who fears God and shuns evil? And still he holds fast to his integrity, although you incited Me against him, to destroy him without cause'" Job 2:3).

"In all this Job did not sin with his lips" (Job 2:10b).

Father, forgive us for broken commitments and unfulfilled vows. We repent today in Jesus Name, and we commit ourselves to be men of our word, men of integrity, men of character. Set a guard over our mouths. Keep watch over the door of our lips, we ask, in Jesus' Name.

CHAPTER 12

Elijah, a Man Who Was Accused Falsely for Being a Troublemaker Among His People

*So Obadiah went to meet Ahab, and told him;
and Ahab went to meet Elijah. Then it happened,
when Ahab saw Elijah, that Ahab said to him, "Is
that you, O troubler of Israel?" And he answered,
"I have not troubled Israel; but you and your
father's house have, in that you have forsaken the
commandments of the LORD, and have followed
the Baals."*

1 Kings 18:16-18

I want to draw a distinction between the subject of this
chapter and what we will see later in Chapter 19 in

regards to persecution that comes from unbelievers. Sadly, some persecution comes from inside the church as well as outside. Ahab was a confessed follower of Yahweh, a child of Abraham, and a fellow Israelite, yet he called the man of God the "troubler of Israel."

It will not be long before some in the church are going to see someone that is burning with the fire of God or bringing the prophetic word of God as a "troublemaker."

"Why can't we just do things like we always have? Why do you have to be so fanatical? What are you trying to accomplish by all your efforts? Who made you a judge over us?" (Exodus 2:14).

Just get ready, Brother, to ruffle the feathers of some roosters in the coop, but go on and love them anyways. It seems so often that when the religious see real anointing, they feel threatened. They may label it as having a lack of discernment or having a "youthful zeal." They may call it pride or simply being "unseasoned," declaring it a "phase" that will soon wear off. Remember David's brother? In 1 Samuel 17:28 when Eliab saw David stirring things up in the camp of God, he got angry and actually accused David of having "pride" and "insolence" in his heart. How ugly it is when there is jealousy and personal agendas involved! How true are James' words, "But if you have bitter envy and self-seeking in your hearts, do not boast and lie against the truth. This wisdom does not descend from above, but *is* earthly, sensual, demonic. For where envy and self-seeking *exist,* confusion and every evil thing *are* there" (James 5:14-16).

When the one under the anointing starts drawing attention to how God is not being honored as He should be and is challenging why others are allowing the enemies of God to taunt the people of God, he should prepare himself to be called a troublemaker, a rabble rouser. If you find yourself in this role, some will rise up and quickly try to "put you in your place." In love and humility, speak the Word of God anyway. Do not take it to heart when your zeal turns some of those in the camp of God off. Remember the words of Paul, "For do I now persuade men, or God? Or do I seek to please men? For if I still pleased men, I would not be a bondservant of Christ" (Galatians 1:10).

Consider what the man healed by Jesus encountered in John 9. This man was stirring up some things by his testimony and people began listening. A religious spirit does not like attention going to others when it fights so hard to maintain its control. Note what the Pharisees say after the man who had been healed made this simple statement of truth, "Now we know that God does not hear sinners; but if anyone is a worshiper of God and does His will, He hears him. Since the world began it has been unheard of that anyone opened the eyes of one who was born blind. If this Man were not from God, He could do nothing" (9:31-33).

Their response was revealing, "You were completely born in sins, and are you teaching us?" Then they cast him out of their midst (9:34).

Be prepared for some similar reactions if you start giving testimony of God's power and glory, for the religious spirit has no current testimony, only knowledge and information. Some in the church (even leaders) that seem so naturally composed will come back spitting venom when they see things out of their "control."

At a Chicago church I was asked to be a youth pastor of a small youth group. I soon discovered that most the few youth we had were doing drugs together! My wife and I prayed and confronted them and by God's grace most of them repented and turned to God. We saw this small, fledgling group grow until we had a room full of worshipers who wanted to seek God's face all night and were going out on the streets of Chicago to share Jesus! One day for an evening service, the church asked our youth group to lead worship. The youth just carried upstairs what they were already doing downstairs, worshiping Jesus with freedom and passion. A couple of them hopped up and down in their excitement in worship (just in the place where they were standing); the others had their hands outstretched to God and singing with all their hearts. At the next deacon's meeting, I had a thing coming to me. One of the deacons was so furious; he said he was "disgusted" and that it actually made him sick. He told me that if it (the hopping) happened again, he would leave. (Interestingly, he had already been talking to others who he said would do the same.) He was blinded at the time to see the victory these youth were walking in; he was blinded from seeing or inquiring about how they were sharing their faith or living in righteousness. He saw this as "troublemaking" to say the least, something that was out of the norm, someone trying to bring fanaticism and emotionalism. God gave me grace to respond with the Word of God (pointing out Michal's reaction to David's dancing in 2 Samuel 6), to hold my tongue and let the Word speak for itself, and to love him. (Love won out; we have remained friends.)

Prepare yourself to respond with patience and love, but also with the Word of God. You may even be cast out, but God will lead those who are longing for His glory, and He will put you in fellowship with others of like mind and spirit.

Father, give us Your heart for the church. Help us to be a voice of truth, but let us say with Paul that we will love those in the church more even if we be loved less. Break the spirit of religion, the pride of man, and the spirit of competition and jealousy and control in the church. Let all recognize that You, Jesus, are the head and that all the attention is to go to You!

Week #2
Discussion questions and points of application

1. Pray for each other, that each man would see how God wants to use them in the strategic position He has placed them to bring the Kingdom of God to their workplace.

2. Pray for each other to be carriers of God's presence, to be those that manifest His glory.

3. How have you stepped out of your comfort zone recently to love someone? How can you be intentional in loving others? From the person who is homeless, to the one who is at the service counter? How are you fulfilling Matthew 25:31-40?

4. Are you obeying the command to "earnestly desire spiritual gifts?" Are you really wanting to be used of God and live a supernatural life or are you making excuses and content to live the life you have now? Are you hungry to see God's glory, His power in and through your life?

5. Who are men who you know who walk in great spiritual authority, and see if you see a connection with how they are men of their word, men of integrity.

6. How can wisdom be used in dealing with those in the Body who are resistant to moves of the Spirit, emotion and zeal? How can we keep the unity of the church to the best of our ability?

7. Pray for each other's families, work, and for opportunities to share Jesus and pray for someone this next week.

Elijah, a Man Who Directly Confronted False Prophets (Even Though Outnumbered)

Now therefore, send and gather all Israel to me on Mount Carmel, the four hundred and fifty prophets of Baal, and the four hundred prophets of Asherah, who eat at Jezebel's table.

1 Kings 18:19

I do not know anyone who likes confrontation. Yet, if we say we love Jesus, it is not optional. For too long there have been too many men who are spineless. Today many will complain and many will talk, but few will act. We do not need men of words, we need men of action. As the expression often attributed to philosopher Edmund Burke says, "The only thing necessary for

~ 95 ~

evil to triumph is for good men to do nothing."

The Word of God must be obeyed fully, not partially.

Jesus said, "Take heed to yourselves. If your brother sins against you, rebuke him; and if he repents, forgive him" (Luke 17:3).

Paul exhorted Timothy as a young pastor, "Those who are sinning rebuke in the presence of all, that the rest also may fear" (1 Timothy 5:20).

Paul says again in 2 Timothy 4:2, "Preach the Word! Be ready in season and out of season. Convince, rebuke, exhort, with all longsuffering and teaching."

Titus also is told, "This testimony is true. Therefore rebuke them sharply, that they may be sound in the faith" (Titus 1:13). Again, in Titus 2:15, "Speak these things, exhort, and rebuke with all authority. Let no one despise you."

In other words, this is a part of the Christian life. Expect it, do it in love, and get over yourself and your fears. Be obedient.

In this chapter we are specifically talking about those who are false prophets. Who are false prophets and teachers? If you are not sure, then really study 2 Peter 2, the Book of Jude, and 1 Timothy 4 again. Here are some noteworthy points from these passages that reveal the attributes of false prophets and teachers:

1. They prohibit things that God blessed (like food and marriage).
2. They love this present world.
3. They will come in secretly.
4. They will be covetous, taking advantage of the people of God to become wealthy.
5. They will live in sin and promote sin.

6. They will despise authority.

7. They will walk in pride and speak with arrogance.

8. They will desire that which is not holy.

9. They will live out the desires of the flesh.

10. Their eyes will be full of desire for sexual sin.

11. They will deceive unstable souls.

12. They may have started with Christ but will forsake the Way.

13. They will be marked with the love of money and be motivated by money.

14. They will boast of great things they have seen or special revelations they have received that are contrary to the Word and the nature of Christ.

15. They will promise liberty but they themselves are slaves to sin.

16. Their end is worse than their beginning.

17. They use the grace of God as an excuse or license for sin.

18. They speak evil against things about which they know nothing.

19. They create a lot of stir and emotion but produce nothing.

20. They are constantly complaining and murmuring.

And obviously, they will speak such things as, "Thus says the Lord," or prophesy things that do not come to pass. If their prophecy does come to pass or they perform some miracle, but they use it to turn hearts away from the Word of God, and from Jesus, they are to be rebuked and rejected (see Deuteronomy 13).

Brother, if you see something you know is against God, but

the one who is claiming it is of God, go to him and rebuke him privately. If it is being done openly and unashamedly, then rebuke such a one publicly. It is time for the prophets of God to arise and speak righteousness in love and humility—even if they stand alone. The cost of not doing so is too great. Many will continue to be led astray if we do not speak out. As someone once said, "If you are on God's side, you will always be in the majority." That is all that matters. God will fill your mouth, so be obedient as Elijah was obedient. You must also be prepared, for your enemy is prepared to counter you. Be filled with the Word of God and with His Spirit, and He will give you victory and, by His grace, draw hearts back to follow the right way.

In 2000, the issue of homosexuality was already upfront and in your face more than ever in America, but it was then, as I remember it, that many churches began to side with the world on this issue. There was a pastor that had gotten some press in the nation, coming from a mainline denominational church, who was saying that the Bible did not condemn homosexuality and that the church needed to open up to this alternative "lifestyle" and accept it. The pastor of the church I was attending at the time (and in which I was serving as a youth pastor) is a man of God. He showed me a pamphlet that was an invitation for all to join in an open forum with this pastor who was saying homosexuality was acceptable in the church. He told me he was not able to go and asked if I would like to go. In fact, the words my pastor said to me were, "Are you willing to go be a prophet for the hour?"

I remember the initial response I felt, one that many can relate to, one of apprehension and nervousness. "Not me. Surely someone else will do it." However, the issue is always for us to ask God what He wants. Being obedient to this, I asked. Sure enough, God said, "Go."

Upon entering the room and as I sat there praying, I thought, "I must be the only one here not in support of this!" I sat there for a while as people gave their "nice" comments and testimonies. They discussed the judgmentalism of others as this pastor "expounded" the Scriptures to explain "what they (the Scriptures) really meant."

I sat and sat, and finally I felt the power of the Holy Spirit come upon me, and I began to tremble. Brother, the Bible says you are to go, and He will give you the words in that hour which you are to speak (Luke 21:14-15). I raised my hand and, with my heart pounding, asked God to speak through me. And He did.

I said something to this effect: "I, among others, I'm sure, have come and have been sent by God to warn you to repent of this heretical teaching. I'm another witness on the road of your life, to warn you to turn from this before it's too late, before you face God one day." I then gave some Scripture references. I'll never forget this man's response. He was calm and prepared (no doubt having seen others like me before). He quickly asked if I believed the Bible to be literal and to be taken in its entirety literally. I replied, "Yes."

Then, knowing there were a lot of women present who could quickly turn against me if I gave the answer he anticipated, asked me, "What about the passages saying women are to be silent in the church?"

Without hesitation, yet not even knowing exactly what I would say, I replied, "If women were not to say anything in church, then why does God say they are to cover their heads while they prophesy?"*

He was silent. He then turned to the people and actually commended me for this response! I stood up and said I again was warning him to turn before it was too late and began to walk out.

Before I left, others began to get angry and say they knew what type I was "those that take the Bible literally," and "I was just like so and so in their family!" Others were silent. When I left, I felt peace in obedience but asked God if there would be any fruit from this. The Spirit of God showed me a man and his son who were sitting in that meeting and showed me that they "heard" and that He had sent me, in part, for them.

We are called to be obedient and speak the truth in love. God brings the change.

Father, give us courage to speak against false teaching and to be a voice of truth amidst voices of deception. Help us to walk in discernment and at all times to be a prophetic voice with the heart to see restoration in Jesus' Name. Let us be reminded—love warns when danger is near.

CHAPTER 14

Elijah, a Man Who Gave a Clear Communication of the Challenge: Who Are You Going to Serve?

So Ahab sent for all the children of Israel, and
gathered the prophets together on Mount Carmel.
And Elijah came to all the people, and said, "How
long will you falter between two opinions? If the
LORD is God, follow him; but if Baal, follow him."
But the people answered him not a word.

1 Kings 18:20-21

"How long will you falter between two opinions?"
I think that is the question of the hour that much of the church in America needs to be asking herself. It is time for the men to rise up and ask that question of the church, having first asked themselves the same question and having taken a strong, determined, and godly position. I grew up with the erroneous

teaching many others have grown up with, that says you can accept Jesus as your Savior, and then perhaps later on you can make Him your Lord. Hello? Where is that in the Bible?

What does the Bible reveal? As Dr. Michael Brown points out in his book Revolution in the Church: Challenging the Religious System with a Call for Radical Change (Published by Chosen Books, 2002), the word "Christian" is mentioned just three times in the New Testament and "believer(s)" only 26 times, but "disciple(s)" appears over 260 times! This is how the people of God were identified in the New Testament, and this is how Jesus identified His own—those who truly followed Him. Disciple.

I appreciate the teaching series of Ray Vander Laan, That the World May Know (Copyright 2000, Focus On The Family, Distributed by Zondervan Publishing House).

Mr. Vander Laan examines how the Western world has largely adopted a Greek model of discipleship rather than the Biblical Hebrew model. The Greek model can be seen in Acts 17.

"For all the Athenians and the foreigners who were there spent their time in nothing else but either to tell or to hear some new thing" (Acts 17:21).

They loved information and always desired more knowledge, identifying it with authority. However, there was often what could be called a divorce between knowledge and character—information without application.

The Hebrew mode, on the other hand asks, "How does this work? How does this apply? How do I walk this out?"

I have heard the observation made that most of the sermons today in many churches are about 90 percent doctrine with only about 10 percent application. Jesus' messages, like Paul's, were about 50 percent doctrine and 50 percent application. Break down the messages of Jesus. Look at the Sermon on the Mount. Look at the letters of Paul. For example, study Ephesians and you will find that chapters 1-3 are doctrine, with chapters 4-6 being application. Other letters have even more application. Even Romans, which may be Paul's most doctrinal letter, has consistent application.

In the Jewish society, the desire of the disciple was to imitate the rabbi. Paul speaks of this in 1 Corinthians 11:1. To be a disciple was to have an intense passion, an intense commitment to be just like the rabbi. This meant even going to bed thinking, "How can I be a better disciple tomorrow?" Basically, the disciple lived with the rabbi, observing everything he did.

However, discipleship is also rooted in community. It is not "me doing my own thing," with no level of accountability.

Understanding, then, the contradiction between the Early Church's model of discipleship verses the current model of seeking knowledge independently of any life-application or strong role-modeling, is it any wonder the church struggles with the attitude that what is done in private by men can often be so different than what is done publicly? Where is the accountability? We hardly even get into each others homes! We rarely share a meal together (outside of an occasional pot lock). How can we demonstrate a biblical culture of love when we hardly even know each other? Anyone can put a mask on for the few minutes of interaction before and after services. We don't even know how to really pray for each other, There is such a disconnect in the church, you can have major crisis in marriages or lives and hardly anyone knows about it until after it blows up. It should never have happened, it should never have gotten to that stage.

"How long will you falter between two opinions?"

Jesus said you cannot serve two masters. John says that if

someone loves the world (in that what is defined as the lust of the eyes and flesh and pride of this life), the love of the Father is not in him. You cannot divorce the Savior from the Lord! He is one and the same! It is time to speak a clear message and challenge the church, declaring the Word of God: to be a friend of the world is to be an enemy of God. It is spiritual adultery!

God will not be shared. He is a jealous lover; if you are not convinced of this, read Hosea again.

God expresses Himself to be no different in His emotions than you are in your own. What if you allowed your wife to be shared with other lovers or how would you feel if your wife "lit up" around other men, but not around you? A friend of mine preached so plainly about this one time. His message was: what if you proposed to a lady you loved, and she said, "I love you, too. I want to marry you, and I'm totally committed to you 360 days out of the year!" You would say, "Wait a minute! There are 365 days a year!" What if she said, "I know, but I have these other 5 boyfriends, we just have this tradition, you know? We just get together these certain days, but the rest of the time I'm yours!" What do you think? Do you want a wife like that?

Now, we are talking about the Holy God of all who redeemed you with His own blood. How is it that so many can say, "God, I'm with you Sunday through Thursday, but Friday and Saturday night—I want that time for...some other things." Or "God, I'll give you these areas of my life, but I'm not ready to give up my television, my movies, and my music (in other words my infatuation with the world)"

God says, "Husbands, love your wives, just as Christ also loved the church and gave Himself for her, that He might sanctify and cleanse her with the washing of water by the word, that He might present her to Himself a glorious church, not having spot or wrinkle or any such thing, but that she should be holy and without blemish" (Ephesians 5:25-27).

We are the Bride of Christ earnestly looking for the return of our heavenly Bridegroom. Not like some betrothed wife playing around with other lovers before her wedding day! We are clothed in white awaiting the return of the King! Jesus warned, "Behold I am coming as a thief. Blessed is he who watches, and keeps his garments, lest he walk naked and they see his shame" (Revelation 16:15).

Brother are you in the place to make a deal with God about to what extent you surrender to Him in your life? The question is, "God, is this pleasing to you or not?" And, if it is not, then get rid of it. It is time to make up your mind. It is time to make a decision. "How long will you waver between two opinions?" Settle it once and for all. Then, go in compassion and wake up others who still think they can separate the Savior from the Lord.

Father, You said that a double-minded man is unstable in all his ways. Make us men of conviction and vision, who walk out this faith with action, not just doctrinal assent. Let us live and preach the truth; as You said, Jesus, unless a man forsakes all he cannot be Your disciple. We give ourselves to be Your disciples, 365 days of the year, 24 hours a day. We put our hand to the plow and will not look back. We build the tower with the knowledge of what it will cost to finish it. We go to war even though we are far out-numbered. We will be counted as Your disciples. In Jesus' Name, we pray.

CHAPTER 15

Elijah, a Man Who Restored the Altar of God (The Restoration of Praise and Worship)

Then Elijah said to the people, "I alone am left a prophet of the LORD; but Baal's prophets are four hundred and fifty men. Therefore let them give us two bulls; and let them choose one bull for themselves, cut it in pieces, and lay it on the wood, but put no fire under it; and I will prepare the other bull, and lay it on the wood, but put no fire under it. Then you call on the name of your gods, and I will call on the name of the LORD; and the God who answers by fire, He is God." So all the people answered and said, "It is well spoken." Now Elijah said to the prophets of Baal, "Choose one bull for yourselves and prepare it first; for you are many; and call on the name of your god, but put no fire under it. So they took the bull which was given them, and they prepared it, and called on the name of Baal from morning even till noon, saying, "O Baal, hear us!" But there was no voice; no one answered. Then they leaped about the altar which they had made. And so it was, at noon, that Elijah mocked them and said, "Cry aloud, for he is a god; either he is meditating, or he is busy, or he is on a journey, or perhaps he is sleeping and must be awakened." So they cried aloud, and cut themselves, as was their custom, with knives and lancets, until the blood gushed out on them. And when midday was past, they prophesied until the time of the offering of the evening sacrifice. But there was no voice; no one answered, no one paid attention. Then Elijah said to all the people, "Come near to me." So all the people came near to him. And he repaired the altar of the LORD that was broken down.

1 Kings 18:22-30

O men, it is time to restore the altars of God! It is time to restore worship! The altar is not just a place of sacrifice, a place of absolute surrender, but also a place of giving God praise and thanks! It is not about us! It is not a performance. It is not creating an atmosphere with stage lights and smoke; it is exalting Yahweh, our Lord Jesus Christ, the King of kings, the lover of our souls, the coming world Ruler, and our heavenly Bridegroom!

It is time we understand what God calls worship and praise. God is sovereign, and He chose the Hebrew language to define praise. The wonderful thing about the Hebrew language is that it so often uses the physical body to bring understanding to the word. Brother, it really does matter what you do with your body! When men came in contact with the glory of God, they were not standing. They were not sitting with their legs crossed, sipping iced tea. They were on their faces!

If the President of our nation—regardless of your opinion of him—were to come into the room, would you just sit there and speak casually to him? No. You would show respect with your body language. Read Romans 13:1-7. (By the way, do you recall which emperor was reigning when Peter wrote his letter? It was Nero (1 Peter 2:13, 14, 17)).

We have adopted the mentality: "I worship God the way I want to." Praise and worship are not to be what we want, but what God desires and defines in His Word as being acceptable to Him. It is not how we think we should show love to God, but how He feels He actually is loved. In fact it is not biblical to call something "praise" if there is no physical response.

Meditate on some of the Hebrew words for "praise" listed below as taken from Strong's Concordance. Ask the Holy Spirit to give you revelation and a clear vision of how your body should respond to what your spirit is saying to God. Then do it—for the glory of God!

8426— Towdah —Expression of thanks, thank offerings, thanksgiving in songs of liturgical worship, hymn, a choir of worshipers, or praise, **an extension of the hands**, a sacrifice of praise. Psalm 50:23

1288 – Barak – To bless (302 times), curse (4 times), **kneel**

down, to bless, to kneel. Psalm 103:1-2

1974 – Hilluwl – Harvest Celebration, to praise, to make merry, rejoicing

1984 – Hallel – to praise, thank, boast, **mad, shine, foolish, rage**, to shine, to boast, **to act clamorously foolish**. Psalm 150

2167 – Zamar – to play music, **to strike with the fingers**, sing psalms, make music, to play a musical instrument. Psalm 57:7

3034 – Yadah – to revere or worship, to praise (53 times), give thanks, to confess, **cast, to throw, to shoot arrows**. Psalm 9:1

4110 – Mahalal – Fame, good reputation, to praise

7623 – Shabach – to address, to pacify, to praise, **triumph**, glory**, to boast,** commend. Psalm 63:3,4.

7321 – Ruuah – shout (23 times), noise (seven times), alarm (four times), cry (four times), triumph (three times), to shout, raise a sound, cry out, give a blast, **to shout a war cry or alarm of battle**. To sound a signal for war or a march. To shout in triumph over enemies. Psalm 47:1,5.

8416 – Tehillah – laudation, hymn, praise, thanksgiving, **praise demanded by qualities or deeds or attributes of God,** act of general or public praise, a song or hymn of praise. Psalm 92:1.

I hear men say, "I'm not the shouting type" or "I'm not into charismatic worship." Really? Is it about you? Yet these same men will not think twice about shouting at a football or basketball game, or shouting at their kids or wife in anger. What hypocrisy.

Look at the sheer number of times things are mentioned in the Bible concerning this, and it will reveal something about God's view on praise and worship:

Missions and evangelism: Maybe you can find 12 times where we are commanded to evangelize or make disciples, yet we know this is central. It is the Great Commission. In contrast, we are commanded to shout at least 65 times, not "if you feel like it", but "Shout!"

Justification by faith: 70 times in Scripture, but we are commanded to give thanks to the Lord at least 135 times.

Sanctification: At least 72 times, but 287 times we are commanded to sing to the Lord! Not "if you can sing" but "Sing to the Lord!"

Baptism: Mentioned all together about 83 times, but we are commanded to rejoice in God 288 times!

The second coming of Jesus: At least 318 times, yet we are commanded to praise the Lord at least 332 times! HalleluYah! God wants us to walk in praise! To walk in rejoicing! To walk in thanksgiving! To shout a war cry to Him! He has triumphed over His enemies! (I am indebted to Pastor Bob Lane for doing the homework on the numbers and bringing the message on praise).

One of the requirements of the priest (remember that God reveals the physical before He reveals the spiritual) in offering the sacrifice to God was at times to remove the kidneys and the intestines of the animal. Why? What was the significance of this to the Jews? These organs were considered the seat of the emotions! They were the place of the most intense emotions, it is the deep belly cry of a mother who has lost her child or shouting with all your strength until you feel it in the pit of your stomach.

God says that belongs to Him! Those deepest emotions are not to be spent on sports or the things of this world, but given to Him in praise. Just as you want your wife to be most passionate for you, God is no different when He is looking at the bride for His beloved Son Jesus! Father, we throw off anything that would compete for our passion and declare that You have our chief affections! You are Who we shout for! You are Who we are passionate for! Forgive us as a church for our hypocrisy and for offering blemished, lame sacrifices and not giving You the best! You are worthy of our very best!

How the devil hates praise, he will fight praise like few other things, and few things stir up and anger a religious spirit more.

The enemy knows that God inhabits praise (Psalm 22:3)

Look at the revivals of the past, and you will see exuberant praise in those revivals. Look at the periods that are cold and dead in the church, and you will see the absence of Biblical praise. The Dark Ages were indeed dark, and the devil took nearly all the instruments of praise out of the church. Basically, all that was left was chanting. However, where the people of God are filled with praise, there is victory, there is freedom and there is joy. It is in the presence of God that fullness of joy is found (Psalm 16:11)!

God tells us to replace the yoke of heaviness with garments of praise (Isaiah 61:3). So many people in the church are battling depression. I believe if we, the church, are in true biblical praise, we will see depression fall off God's people like someone throwing off a backpack full of rocks!

Praise and worship bring us to a place of triumph. In fact, God's Word declares that we "triumph in His praise" (Psalm 106:47)!

People will try to play the card that it is "not their personality to praise like this." Brothers, I, by nature, am a quiet person, just ask my parents. I grew up extremely quiet, but I learned when it comes to what God wants from my life, that it's not about my personal preferences. It is about God receiving praise, and when I began to praise God according to the Hebrew words for praise, it changed me. Look at the Chinese. They are a reserved people, much more unemotional than Westerners. Yet, what will you see in the underground Chinese churches? You will see shouting, yelling, passion, "all for Jesus," Holy Spirit-filled worship and praise. Does that mean we shout all the time, every time? Of course not, there is a time for being quiet before the Lord, a time to be still and know that He is God (Psalm 46). However, it is time to restore worship in the church to its fullness, understanding what the Word teaches and models, and it begins with you. Then you need to model it to your family. They need to see that passionate praise in you. That is when you will not have your kids thinking "Hypocrite," in the church because they only see you getting excited and shouting about something of no eternal value. They will stop looking at rock concerts and saying to themselves, "Why are they more passionate about this then anything I've seen in the church?" God might be asking the same question.

It is time to rebuild the altars to the one true God.

Someone may be quick to quote, "Let all things be done in decency and order" to which I say, "Amen." But let us do the ALL THINGS first, and then we can also do them in order. Let us return to the full teaching of the Bible, which supersedes culture. The problem is that many leaders in the church get nervous at passion because they themselves have not gone to that point in their personal worship.

Where does passionate worship come from? I believe (see Luke 7:36-50 as a reference) passionate worship (that will worship even in the face of religious persecution or judgmentalism) comes when you have a revelation of God's holiness, your own sin, and how great a debt has been forgiven you by God. When you see how great an expanse God crossed to save you from the wrath to come and with what great love He loved you when you were not even searching for Him, you will praise Him with all your strength! Brother, you were bound for hell fire—forever—and God redeemed you by His own blood, what is there not to shout about in that? You are on your way to heaven, forever, by the grace of God, to be in His presence forever in the New Jerusalem. How can you not lift up your hands in worship?

By the way, you are commanded to dance too (Psalm 150).

Father, we will praise You with all our hearts! Let our bodies bear witness of this truth! We will triumph in Your praise! Let the praise of the Lord be continually in our mouths! Even if it feels like we are in a prison cell, let us praise You! You are worthy!

CHAPTER 16

Elijah, a Man Driven By Pure Motives

And Elijah took twelve stones, according to the number of the tribes of the sons of Jacob, unto whom the word of the LORD had come, saying, "Israel shall be your name." Then with the stones he built an altar in the name of the LORD; and he made a trench around the altar large enough to hold two seahs of seed. And he put the wood in order, cut the bull in pieces, and laid it on the wood, and said, "Fill four water pots with water, and pour it on the burnt sacrifice and on the wood." Then he said, "Do it a second time," and they did it a second time; and he said, "Do it a third time," and they did it a third time. So the water ran all around the altar; and he also filled the trench with water. And it came to pass, at the time of the offering of the evening sacrifice, that Elijah the prophet came near and said, "LORD God of Abraham, Isaac,

and Israel, let it be known this day that you are
God in Israel and I am your servant, and that I
have done all these things at Your word. Hear me,
O LORD, hear me, that this people may know that
you are the LORD God, and that You have turned
their hearts back to You again."

1 Kings 18:31-37

So he said, "I have been very zealous for the
LORD God of hosts; for the children of Israel have
forsaken Your covenant, torn down Your altars,
and killed Your prophets with the sword. I alone
am left; and they seek to take my life."

1 Kings 19:10

M<u>o·tive</u> (noun) – A reason for doing something, especially, one that is hidden or not obvious. From the Latin word motivus, from movere "to move" (The New Oxford American Dictionary).

The motivation of why you do something is everything. Why you "do what you do" will eventually be revealed to everyone. It may take time, but it will eventually come out—of your mouth. "For of the abundance of the heart the mouth speaks," Jesus declared (Matthew 12:34).

This was revealed in the sorcerer, Simon, in Acts 8. His motive of wanting power was an abomination to God, and Peter used strong words to rebuke him. James said that the reason some prayer is not answered is that the motive is wrong (James 4). You can pray and fast for hours and days, but if your motive is wrong, you are just blowing wind and wasting energy; your prayers will go no higher than the ceiling.

Look at the heart of Elijah. His one motive, his heart's desire, is the honoring of Yahweh's Name. It is for the people of God to really know that He is the LORD and that He would have their hearts. That is to be our cry: that Jesus is the center.

I love what has been quoted concerning Charles Spurgeon's preaching, someone came away from his message and didn't say, "What an amazing preacher," but rather, "What an amazing God that preacher serves!" HalleluYah!

Elijah did not do what he did so that people could see what a great man he was or so that he could receive any credit, fame, or to win a popularity poll. He did it for the glory of God! That was his only motivation. It was not about Elijah. He was Jealous for the Name of God to be glorified. He was troubled that God was not receiving the praise due Him.

Who are we drawing attention to? Is all the glory going to God, or are we putting our hand in the glory, receiving some of the credit?

Are we jealous for the Lord God of Hosts? Does it bother us that His name is not being lifted up as it should be? Does it bother us that we have fallen so far from the book of Acts where it records the fear that came upon the people as they were convicted to hold the church in high respect? This was not for respect for respect's sake, but because they knew God was in their midst!

Are we unsettled at the complacency around us? Perhaps we even see it in our own lives? Are we troubled at the conversations that dominate a lot of Christian men's circles? Does it bother us that statistics now show that most Christians in America give around 2 percent of their money to God while sitting on bank accounts that make the vast majority of the world's population look like paupers?

Does it bother you that most Christian men will think nothing of spending hundreds, even thousands, of dollars on entertainment and yet give so little for the evangelization of the world? That research concludes that about 2% of the evangelical church shares the Gospel?

It is time that you check your motives—now. What are you living for? Why are you going to church? Why are you praying? Why go evangelize? Why do you give? (This constant message in some circles of "seed giving" in order to get back more should turn our stomachs!) We need to let the Holy Spirit search our hearts now, to reveal if there are ulterior motives, that we would repent and make certain that whether [we] eat or drink, or whatever [we] do, [we] do all to the glory of God" (1 Corinthians 10:31).

The purity of our motivation will also often reveal how far we will go in obeying the Spirit's call. It exposes how quickly we can be discouraged or even turn back to the ways of the world when confronted with trials and tribulation.

If you have not heard the message "Ten Shekels and a Shirt" by Paris Reidhead, you need to. It will impact you profoundly and could change your life as it probes this issue of our motive for ministry and people's motives for coming to Jesus. At the time of this writing, an audio recording of it is available online by searching "Paris Reidhead" and the sermon title.

May we fulfill the Law and the Prophets—by the power of the Holy Spirit that lives within us—as we love the Lord our God with all our heart, soul, mind, and strength and love our neighbor as ourselves. O God, may we have pure hearts. Let there be nothing but pure motivation for anything and everything we do for you. Father, reveal if there is any motivation in our heart that is self-seeking. May all we do be for the honor and glory of Your Name.

Our faith is in You to purify our motive, for we acknowledge that the heart is deceitful, but You are greater than our hearts. Thank You for giving us undivided hearts that fear Your Name, thank You for hearing this prayer in Jesus' Name.

CHAPTER 17

Elijah, a Man Who Destroyed Enemies of God

And Elijah said to them, "Seize the prophets of
Baal! Do not let one of them escape!" So they
seized them; and Elijah brought them down to the
Brook Kishon and executed them there.

1 Kings 18:40

I remember reading the testimony of a church many years ago that wanted to establish a room for the men of the church to use for prayer. It had been brought to the attention of the pastor of that church that most often it is women who decorate the churches, so there tends to be more of the floral themes, softer colors, and the interior decorator touch (and we are thankful for the beauty they bring!). He wanted to see how the men would decorate this room of prayer, so he gave them the freedom to decorate it any way they wanted. What did they do? They bought swords and shields and pieces of armor and mounted them on the walls! It looked like a room ready for battle! When they entered it to pray, there were physical reminders that they were in a war! They were to fight in prayer! We are not seeing much of this today because the men are largely missing from the prayer house.

"For though we walk in the flesh, we do not war according to the flesh. For the weapons of our warfare are not carnal but mighty in God for pulling down strongholds, casting down arguments and every high thing that exalts itself against the knowledge of God, bringing every thought into captivity to the obedience of Christ" (2 Corinthians 10:3-5).

This is the language of the New Testament!

"For if you live according to the flesh you will die; but if by the Spirit you put to death the deeds of the body, you will live" (Romans 8:13).

"Therefore put to death your members which are on the earth: fornication, uncleanness, passion, evil desire, and covetousness, which is idolatry" (Colossians 3:5).

"Finally, my brethren, be strong in the Lord and in the power of His might. Put on the whole armor of God, that you may be able to stand against the wiles of the devil. For we do not wrestle against flesh and blood, but against principalities, against powers, against the rulers of the darkness of this age, against spiritual hosts of wickedness in the heavenly places. Therefore take up the whole armor of God, that you may be able to withstand in the evil day, and having done all, to stand. Stand therefore, having girded your waist with truth, having put on the breastplate of righteousness, and having shod your feet with the preparation of the gospel of peace; above all, taking the shield of faith with which you will be able to quench all the fiery darts of the wicked one. And take the helmet of salvation, and the sword of the Spirit, which is the word of God;

praying always with all prayer and supplication in the Spirit, being watchful to this end with all perseverance and supplication for all the saints" (Ephesians 6:10-18).

"This charge I commit to you, son Timothy, according to the prophecies previously made concerning you, that by them you may wage the good warfare" (1 Timothy 1:18).

"Fight the good fight of faith, lay hold on eternal life, to which you were also called and have confessed the good confession in the presence of many witnesses" (1 Timothy 6:12).

"You therefore must endure hardship as a good soldier of Jesus Christ. No one engaged in warfare entangles himself with the affairs of this life, that he may please him who enlisted him as a soldier" (2 Timothy 2:3-4).

"I have fought the good fight, I have finished the race, I have kept the faith" (2 Timothy 4:7).

"You have not yet resisted to bloodshed, striving against sin" (Hebrews 12:4).

"Beloved, while I was very diligent to write to you concerning our common salvation, I found it necessary to write to you exhorting you to contend earnestly for the faith which was once for all delivered to the saints" (Jude 3).

Look how Paul addresses a fellow believer:

"To the beloved Apphia, Archippus our fellow soldier, and to the church in your house" (Philemon 2).

Look at the promises of Jesus to those in the church are to those who "overcome" (Revelation 2:7, 2:11, 2:17, 2:26, 3:5, 3:12, 3:21).

We overcome the enemy by the blood of the Lamb, the word of our testimony and **if we love not our lives even to death** (Revelation 12:11).

Do you walk in this biblical reality? The life of a disciple of Jesus is not a playground; it is a battleground. I think that we greatly underestimate how much the enemy is working. If we had a greater understanding, we would be praying and rebuking more.

I recall another testimony of Pastor Yongghi Cho from South Korea. He shared about a night when he came home very depressed, wanting to leave the church and to give up pastoring. He transparently shared that as he came into his house, many things annoyed him. He confessed that when he came into his bedroom, his wife's light snore annoyed him and that he did not think she was pretty (and on and on). Suddenly, the Spirit revealed to him that he was under attack. He went into another room and prayed out, according to how Jesus taught us to pray, "Deliver me from evil!" Then, he said the window in his room suddenly shook and he felt completely different. He began to worship and thank God for allowing him to be a pastor. As he went back into his bedroom, he loved the sound his wife was making and remarked to himself, "What a beautiful woman my wife is!" His whole attitude and perspective were changed!

How many times do you think your attitude towards things, people, or circumstances is being affected by the enemy's influence and an attack on your life?

"Therefore, <u>submit</u> to God. <u>Resist</u> the devil and he will flee from you" (James 4:7, emphasis mine).

<u>Remember in this friend, our spiritual authority is directly linked to the measure of your being surrendered and submitted to God!</u> You must make sure your body, mind, and soul are submitted to God. You must make sure your time, is submitted to God; your work, your relationships, the money you have, your future, your reputation, are <u>all</u> submitted to God. Then there will be true

authority resist the enemy, and he <u>will</u> flee!

We need to take very seriously that we are in a fight and the enemy will fight to get us to focus on ourselves, our circumstances, or <u>anything</u> to keep us from praying for God's Kingdom to come and from going out to advance His Kingdom!

God has given us spiritual weapons, and we need to use them!

It was when the men of Israel gave a great shout to God (as in Joshua 6:20) or a shout of praise (as in 2 Chronicles 20:22) that the enemy was defeated and the Lord wrought a great victory!

When is the last time you heard a group of men shout a war cry out to God in prayer? A war cry of victory over their families, over their churches, and over their communities? I will state it again, many men will shout at a sports game, but it is time for men to rise up and give a shout to God in praise and to cry out for revival and for many souls to come to Jesus.

There was a realization some time ago that at a point in American history when many able-bodied men left for war and others began to work seven days a week because of the industrial age, the church began to be filled largely by women. As a result, messages catered more to the women, the young, and the elderly. More of the nurturing heart of the Father, the gentle, calming side of God Who embraces us and puts us on His "lap," began to be preached to these congregations. Now, all of this is Biblical and needs to be preached!

However, we must reclaim the full revelation of God.

Isaiah 42:13 declares, "The LORD shall go forth like a mighty man; He shall stir up His zeal like a man of war. He shall cry out, yes, shout aloud; He shall prevail against His enemies."

This is our God!

Lest you think this is only in the Old Testament, just look at the book of Revelation. Look again at the coming of our Lord Jesus and the armies of heaven! The One that leads us to victory! Fight, men of God, on your knees. Wrestle and get the victory, for Jesus is worthy!

Father, lead us on to spiritual victory. Teach us how to fight in the Spirit and to walk in spiritual alertness, discerning the schemes of the devil. Let Your men be found in the prayer house in great numbers shouting Your praise, calling on Your promises, and entering Your bleeding heart for the church and the nations. Raise up Your army, O God, in Jesus' Name!

(Pastor Cho's testimony is taken from a video on his teaching, "Praying though the "Our Father" prayer of Matthew 6" in a local church)

CHAPTER 18

Elijah, a Man Who Persevered in Prayer

Then Elijah said to Ahab, "Go up, eat and drink; for there is the sound of abundance of rain." So Ahab went up to eat and drink. And Elijah went up to the top of Carmel; then he bowed down on the ground, and put his face between his knees, and said to his servant, "Go up now, look toward the sea." So he went up and looked, and said, "There is nothing." And seven times he said, "Go again."
1 Kings 18:41-43

"Believe me, to pray with all your heart and strength, with reason and the will, to believe vividly that God will listen to your voice through Christ, and, verily to do the thing that pleaseth thereupon—this is the last, the greatest achievement of the Christian's warfare upon the earth. Teach us to pray, O Lord." — Samuel Coleridge

"Those who have left the deepest impression on this sin-cursed earth have been men and women of prayer."—D.L. Moody

"The greatest thing anyone can do for God and man is pray. It is not the only thing; but it is the chief thing. The great people of the earth today are the people who pray. I do not mean those who talk about prayer; nor those who say they believe in prayer; nor yet those who can explain about prayer; but I mean those people who take time to pray." – S.D. Gordon

"Elijah was a man skilled in the art of prayer, who altered the course of nature, strangled the economy of a nation, prayed and the fire fell, prayed and the rain fell. We need rain, rain, rain! The churches are so parched that seed cannot germinate. Our altars are dry, with no hot tears of penitents. Oh for an Elijah! His whole life is summed up in two words, "He prayed." (James 5:17) —Leonard Ravenhill

Seven times Elijah prayed. He could have given up after the third time, or the fifth, but he did not. He persevered and persevered until the answer came.

This is how Jesus taught us to pray in Luke 11:

> *And He said to them, "Which of you shall have a friend, and go to him at midnight and say to him, 'Friend, lend me three loaves; for a friend of mine has come to me on his journey, and I have nothing to set before him'; and he will answer from within and say, 'Do not trouble me; the door is now shut, and my children are with me in bed; I cannot rise and give to you'? I say to you, though he will not rise and give to him because he is his friend, yet*

because of his persistence he will rise and give him
as many as he needs.

"So I say to you, ask, and it will be given to you;
seek, and you will find; knock, and it will be
opened to you. For everyone who asks receives,
and he who seeks finds, and to him who knocks it
will be opened.
If a son asks for bread from any father among you,
will he give him a stone? Or if he asks for a fish,
will he give him a serpent instead of a fish? Or if
he asks for an egg, will he offer him a scorpion? If
you then, being evil, know how to give good gifts to
your children, how much more will your heavenly
Father give the Holy Spirit to those who ask Him!"

Jesus taught us to persevere in prayer and the context in
which we should be most persevering is in prayer for the Holy
Spirit, that we may have complete dependence on the Holy Spirit
in everything. Are you obeying this, Brother? Ask now, seek now,
and knock now. God's promises are "yes and amen."

Jesus taught the same thing in Luke 18:

Then He spoke a parable to them, that men always
ought to pray and not lose heart, saying: "There
was in a certain city a judge who did not fear God
nor regard man. Now there was a widow in that
city; and she came to him, saying, 'Get justice
for me from my adversary.' And he would not for
a while; but afterward he said within himself,

'Though I do not fear God nor regard man, yet because this widow troubles me I will avenge her, lest by her continual coming she weary me.'" Then the Lord said, "Hear what the unjust judge said. And shall God not avenge His own elect who cry out day and night to Him, though He bears long with them? I tell you that He will avenge them speedily. Nevertheless, when the Son of Man comes, will He really find faith on the earth?"

We have two choices: we will either lose heart or we will persevere in prayer. That is it. Which will you choose in the time of testing and trial? Jesus taught us to persevere in prayer. This is what demonstrates faith. This is going to be a mark of this generation. We are not going to give up! We are going to keep knocking until the Lord responds, until the cloud of His glory comes. Jesus equates perseverance in prayer with faith. Without faith it is **impossible** to please God (Hebrews 11:6).

This is such an unfamiliar experience for so many in this microwave, instant gratification, and click-a-button generation. The attention span of many Americans is hardly more than a few seconds many times. We talk about tithing money, but what about tithing our time (ten percent would be just under two and a half hours)? I think many would hear the same words Jesus spoke to Peter, "Simon, are you sleeping? Could you not watch <u>one hour</u>?" (Mark 14:37). If we dedicated just 15 minutes to solid prayer time in many of our Sunday morning church services, I believe most people would not know what to do. If the leaders are not accustomed to doing it in their private times, how can they model to others how to have extended times of prayer?

So many of our prayer meetings are really "sermonettes" with some prayer covering the prayer list at the end. If you said, "Let's pray until we receive an answer or a sense of breakthrough on one of these prayer needs," people might look at you as if you had two heads or get annoyed at the thought that the prayer time might go over the appointed "hour." We reveal how much we really want a prayer to be answered (or believe it will be) by how much we give ourselves to pray to God for it. Are we easily distracted or dissuaded? Then we cannot possibly want that prayer answered like we may think we do or talk like we do.

However, those who have experienced extended times in intercession know what it means to experience the breakthrough. They know what it means to "pray until you've prayed." They know the **power** of prayer! They know that it is one of the mightiest weapons and privileges God has given us!

I can personally testify with many others that it is when I have been tenacious and have pressed in, in prayer, that I have seen the greatest miracles and experienced God's glory in the most wonderful ways. God responds to the hungry—to the desperate. Read again the accounts of the miracles of Jesus and the stories Jesus wanted to be recorded in His Word. What do you see? Read of the woman who despised shame and embarrassment to get to Jesus at Simon's house (Luke 7) and of blind Bartimeus refusing to be denied when people told him to be quiet. He received his healing as a result (Mark 10:46-52). Read again of the Phoenician woman crying out and the disciples telling Jesus to send her away. Even when Jesus appeared to say no, she kept persevering until He exclaimed, "O woman, great is your faith!" (Matthew 15:22-28). Read of the woman with the issue of blood (Luke 8:43-48) or the ten lepers (Luke 17:12-19) and on and on. The Lord wanted these people's stories recorded in His eternal word: those that persevered, those that were desperate, those that saw no other option, and those that would not be denied. God is speaking, but are we listening?

We will see such perseverance when we, like Jacob facing Esau, realize that there is no other option. When we think there are other options (perhaps our own efforts and abilities, or technology, or our latest "strategy"), we will not take this persevering, prevailing prayer seriously. We must see that we must give it all, that it is time to completely give ourselves to God and to totally depend upon **Him**. We must put ourselves in a position such that God is our only answer, our only hope. We need to stop praying prayers that we can accomplish, rather than prayers only God can fulfill! God likes this kind of attitude and position. Are you willing to go to this place? Are you willing to be in a place of risk that says, "it's all or nothing?" Are you willing to press in? Nothing is stopping you; shut yourself in with God until you sense a breakthrough in your heart. Then continue to abide in the spirit of prayer.

It is for this reason that we specifically built a house of prayer in Guinea Bissau. The structure of the building is based on the tabernacle of the Old Testament. We understand that God's desire is for the fire on His altar to never go out (Leviticus 6:13). We want to be those who will take His invitation seriously to pray and not give Him rest day or night until He establishes what He has promised. We are looking to establish prayer twenty-four hours a day, 7 days a week, knowing that the spread of the Gospel and national revival are directly linked to the persevering prayers of God's saints. There is no other way; there is no other option. It comes as no surprise that God is opening supernatural doors and that we are seeing souls come to Jesus. We have seen doors open to preach His Word in the military, prisons, hospitals, radio and open air. It starts in prayer; it always has, and it always will.

It is for this reason when we were in Senegal, an Islamic stronghold, that we saw fruit come quickly, for there were 30 men committed to pray and fast every day for us (a two brothers per day rotation). How much we will see happen if God's people will really persevere in prayer and not give up or be distracted!

Jesus, You revealed much to Your disciples in response to their asking, "Lord, teach us how to pray." Let us apply that revelation to our lives. We need your grace to persevere in prayer and to walk by faith and not by sight. O God, strengthen us to pray by Your Spirit. We do not know how to pray as we ought. Spirit of God, help us to pray. We ask this in faith, in Jesus' Name.

Week #3
Discussion questions and points of application

1. Describe a time you had to confront someone for something wrong they did. What do you think you could learn from that experience? What would you do differently? How can you use the brotherhood to hold you accountable in being a truth speaker and taking a stand for righteousness and not being a part of the silent majority?

2. Who's the Lord of your life? How does that reveal itself in day-to-day living? When is the last time you intentionally opened your home up to have brothers and sisters in Christ in it to fellowship or share a meal? How are you intentionally seeking to create/ establish biblical community?

3. Is your praise biblical? If you are meeting in a place with the freedom to shout, give a shout of praise to God together. Bring that praise back to your house, whether by CD's or by an instrument. Build an altar of praise with your family or by yourself to the King of glory!

4. Simply ask the Holy Spirit to reveal if there are any impure motives in your walk with God. Ask Him to fill you with purity of heart and motive, that all you would do, and say, would be for the glory of His Name.

5. Give a war cry of victory over your family, over your church and over where God has placed you to reveal His Kingdom in and through you.

6. What ways are you distracted from persevering in prayer? What is worthy of you to persevere in prayer for? Keep a journal of those prayer requests, and persevere until you record God's answer.

CHAPTER 19

Elijah, a Man Who Faced Persecution

Then it came to pass the seventh time, that he said, "There is a cloud, as small as a man's hand, rising out of the sea!" So he said, "Go up, say to Ahab, 'Prepare your chariot, and go down before the rain stops you.'" Now it happened in the meantime that the sky became black with clouds and wind, and there was a heavy rain. So Ahab rode away and went to Jezreel. Then the hand of the LORD came upon Elijah; and he girded up his loins and ran ahead of Ahab to the entrance of Jezreel. And Ahab told Jezebel all that Elijah had done, and how he had executed all the prophets with the sword. Then Jezebel sent a messenger to Elijah, saying, "So let the gods do to me, and more also, if I do not make your life as the life of one of them by tomorrow about this time. And when he saw that, he arose and ran for his life, and went

to Beersheba, which belongs to Judah, and left his
servant there. But he himself went a day's journey
into the wilderness, and came and sat down under
a broom tree. And he prayed that he might die, and
said, "It is enough! Now, LORD, take my life, for I
am no better than my fathers!"

1 Kings 18:44-19:1

Christ's whole life was a cross and martyrdom—yet do you seek rest and joy for yourself? You are deceived if you seek any other thing than to suffer tribulations; for this whole mortal life is full of miseries and marked on every side with crosses. The higher a person has advanced in the Spirit, so much the heavier crosses he often finds. Nevertheless, this man, though in so many ways afflicted, is not without refreshing comfort, for he understands that great benefit is accrued to him by the bearing of his own cross. All the burden of tribulation is turned into the confidence of divine comfort." —Thomas à Kempis

This is a promise: people are going to be angry at the word of righteousness and at being told they are to have <u>complete</u> devotion to the God of the Bible. This is what the Word of God says, "<u>All</u> who desire to live godly in Christ Jesus <u>will</u> suffer persecution" (2 Timothy 3:12). So, if you are not facing persecution, **there is a problem**. You are not a threat to the devil's kingdom. You are either not living a godly life, Brother, or you are not proclaiming the Gospel of Jesus Christ. We should <u>expect</u> persecution, rather than being surprised by it, not griping and whining… saying "they looked at me funny" or "they said mean things to me." We need to return to normal Christianity. According to the Bible, it is not normal to not face persecution! Yet, in most Western churches, if you face persecution, something is wrong with you! "You're not being sensitive enough; you need to do more friendship evangelism." Jesus told us plainly we would be hated as His disciples, and He said in that context, "These things I have spoken to you, **that you should not be made to stumble**" (emphasis mine) (John 16:1).

We need to be teaching this again in the Western Church. It is not being taught in most assemblies, so when people begin to be persecuted, they shut up and become gripped in fear and trying to be politically correct. Peter said that being persecuted for righteousness sake is actually evidence that the spirit of glory rests on your life!

"If you are reproached for the name of Christ, blessed are you, for the Spirit of glory and of God rests upon you. On their part He is blasphemed, but on your part He is glorified" (1 Peter 4:14).

Jesus even gives a clear warning to those compromisingly wanting to be accepted by all, "Woe to you when all men speak well of you, for so did their fathers to the false prophets" (Luke 6:26).

"If you were of the world, the world would love its own. Yet because you are not of the world, but I chose you out of the world, therefore the world hates you" (John 15:19).

"I have given them Your word; and the world has hated them because they are not of the world, just as I am not of the world" (John 17:14).

I encourage you to do your own study of how persecution is considered biblically normal in the life of a disciple of Jesus:

Matthew 5:10-11, 16-18, 23-25, 34-36, 24:8-10, Mark 10:29-31, 13:9-13, Luke 9:22, 21:12-15, John 15:18-25, 16:33,

Acts 4:1-3, 6:10-13, 7:56-60, 8:1, 12:1-4, 13:45, 50-52, 14:2, 4-7, 19, 21,22, 16:19-24, 17:4-10, 13, 18:12-13, 19:9, 23, 30, 20:22-23, 21:13, 30-36, 22:22-24, 23:10-12, 25:7 Romans 8:35-36, 12:18-19, 1 Corinthians 4:11-13, 16:8-9, 2 Corinthians 4:8-13, 6:4-10, 11:23-28, 12:9-10, Galatians 6:17, Ephesians 3:1, 13, 4:1, Philippians 1:7, 13-18, 21, 3:10-11, Colossians 4:18, 1 Thessalonians 1:6, 2:2, 14-15, 2 Thessalonians 1:4-5, 1 Timothy 4:10, 2 Timothy 1:12, 2:9-13, Philemon 9-10, Hebrews 5:8-9, 10:33-34, 11:35-40, 12:2-3, 1 Peter 2:20-23, 4:16-19, 5:10, Revelation 2:13, 6:9-11.

What is to be our response?

1. We are to rejoice, knowing there is a reward in heaven (Matthew 5:12, Revelation 2:8-10).

2. We should rejoice because we are counted worthy to suffer with Jesus (Acts 5:40-42).

3. We should rejoice because we are filling up that which is left of the afflictions of Christ (Colossians 1:24).

4. We should rejoice simply because we are partakers of Christ's suffering and it will be all be worth it when He

appears (1 Peter 4:13-14). God says you are blessed.

What is our responsibility in and through persecution?
We are:

1. Not to fear our persecutors (Matthew 10:26-31).

2. To make a bold confession (Matthew 10:32,33).

3. To love Jesus supremely (Matthew 10:37-40).

4. To bless those who persecute us (Romans 12:14).

5. To pray for those who persecute us and to love them (Matthew 5:44).

6. To look for ways to do good to them (Romans 12:20-21).

7. To not be ashamed of the testimony of God or those who are persecuted (2 Timothy 1:7-8).

8. To not revile back but to commit ourselves to Him who judges righteously (1 Peter 2:23).

9. To make sure we are being persecuted for the right reason! (1 Peter 3:13-17).

One thing that is absolutely astounding is how much the church wants to be accepted by the world. Some feel called to apologize on behalf of others who are preaching the word of righteousness (I am speaking of those preachers of righteousness who are speaking in love, and not pride or hate). Walk in holiness and love, and preach the Word, but stop trying to apologize or shrink away before others who are mocking. The cross is foolishness to those who are perishing, but to us who are being saved it is the power of God (1 Corinthians 1:18).

Paul says again in 1 Corinthians, in chapter 2 verse 14, that "the natural man does not receive the things of the Spirit of God, for they are foolishness to him; nor can he know them, because they are spiritually discerned." Why then are so many in the church trying to get natural men to know the things of the Spirit? They need the Gospel—to be born again—then they can spiritually discern God's Word. Brothers, it is time to count the cost. We need to stop being so concerned about our reputation and be concerned instead about advancing the Kingdom of God and being faithful to preach the Word, to evangelize, and to live a life that is set apart and that can be used in whatever way He wants (2 Timothy 2:20-21).

My wife had the honor of being used to lead a woman to Christ from a Muslim background. When this woman came to Katie in tears, saying that her husband threatened to take the children away if she followed Jesus, Katie told her, as she wept with her, that this was the cross she had to bear. She had to make the decision: Christ or her children. The woman responded, "Yes," for she knew she would rather be in the truth and her soul be saved than to bow to persecution and deny the One Who died for her. The threat was made real. Her husband took her children from her and she was severely persecuted and threatened. Yet she held firmly to Jesus.

Later, by the power of God, her children were restored to her. Since then, she has seen many breakthroughs in the lives of those who fought her so vehemently. Recently, she told Katie that the way some missionaries were presenting the Gospel in the area where she lives was to tell them that Jesus would give them peace and blessing and joy — without mentioning persecution! She said that she saw many of the Muslims, after making a profession of faith but then faced with persecution, become disillusioned. They told her that they felt as if they had been lied to and they actually despised the missionaries in their hearts, for they felt deceived by them. This was not the way of Jesus and His teachings! The church of the West is exporting a weak, shallow Gospel devoid of the message of persecution because the Western church is not being persecuted! There are no excuses! It is time to return to biblical Christianity! I encourage you to read <u>The Overcomers</u> by Richard Wurmbrand to get a better view of modern biblical Christianity.

I have seen many come to Jesus who then faced much persecution. What would they think if they saw timidity in me or saw me apologizing for their suffering? No, when I see them persecuted I pray with them but point them to the Word and to our chief example, Jesus Christ, and they press on. The result? Their faith is strong and unshakable, and they have revealed their heart to be "good soil," not the shallow, rocky soil Jesus spoke about in

Matthew 13 concerning the Kingdom of God.

Father, we embrace the Cross. We embrace Your will and recognize that it includes persecution. Make our foreheads like flint as our hearts burn with Your love. Let us bless those who curse us and pray for those who persecute us or despitefully use us, in Jesus Name.

CHAPTER 20

Elijah, a Man Who Mentored

Then LORD said to him: "Go, return on your way to the Wilderness of Damascus; and when you arrive, anoint Hazael as king over Syria. Also, you shall anoint Jehu the son of Nimshi as king over Israel. And Elisha the son of Shaphat of Abel Meholah you shall anoint as prophet in your place. It shall be that whoever escapes the sword of Hazael, Jehu will kill; and whoever escapes the sword of Jehu, Elisha will kill."

1 Kings 19:15-19

So he departed from there, and found Elisha the son of Shaphat, who was plowing with twelve yoke of oxen before him, and he was with the twelfth. Then Elijah passed by him and threw his mantle on him.

1 Kings 19:19

Now the sons of the prophets that were at Bethel came out to Elisha, and said to him, "Do you know

that the LORD will take away your master from
over you today? And he said, "Yes, I know; keep
silent!"

2 Kings 2:3

And so it was, when they had crossed over, that
Elijah said to Elisha, "Ask! What may I do for
you, before I am taken away from you?" Elisha
said, "Please, let a double portion of your spirit
be upon me."

2 Kings 2:9

Another attribute of those in the Elijah Generation is that they will be "disciplers;" they will be those who pour into the lives of other men and who multiply themselves. It would have been easy for Elijah to finish his work and go on to God, but it is much better to make a disciple. That is leaving a legacy. Notice, that, like his mentor, Elisha forsook all for the calling of God. Everything in the Kingdom begets itself. God wants us to take what we have received and give it away. Jesus said, "Freely you have received, freely give" (Matthew 10:8). God wants to take our experiences, to take our testimonies, to take the things we have been taught and to pour them into another life. That way they can go further than we have gone because they do not have to take as much time to learn those same lessons, but they gain they can gain the same knowledge. Those testimonies and experiences can; fuel the faith, increase vastness of the vision and deepen the determination of the one being discipled. That is one of the beautiful things about discipleship. It also can save you a lot of money and a lot of time! As in a relay race, we are to pass the baton, and just like the relay races, the runners should be getting progressively faster until that final runner looks as though he is flying! It is to cross that finish line, to be a part of the last generation before the coming of Jesus!

We are to invest in others' lives. It is wrong to sit on what you have received and not to give it away! God wants you to pour into another man, disciple him, and then say, "Run! Run! Run for the prize!" He wants you to encourage him, to remind him, "Make your life significant, you only have one opportunity, one chance." Our lives are but a vapor. You need to remind your disciple that one day he will stand before God to give an account of the talents that were entrusted to him. You need to remind him to maintain an eternal perspective, to have one eye on heaven and the other on hell. You need to exhort him to throw off the sin, the things that entangle and run the race with his eyes fixed on Jesus (Hebrews 12:1-2).

There are few things that are more wonderful than seeing a life that you have poured into running for the glory of God. Few things are more rewarding or more joyous! John said it himself, "I have no greater joy than to hear that my children walk in truth" (3 John 1:4). Have you experienced this?

A young man comes to mind who I was privileged to see come to Jesus and to disciple. Seeing him now using the gifts God has given him for the glory of God, seeing him lead others to Jesus, seeing him walk with God, seeing him get the vision—what joy! To see him running—O HalleluYah!

God led us to start a discipleship center in Guinea Bissau with the saints of God who prayed and gave to see it established. What a joy it is to see men I have poured into for 3 months, to see their hunger increase, to see them lead others to Jesus, to see them lay hands on the sick and see them healed, to see them cast out demons, to see them lead. There is nothing else that can be compared to experiencing that investment into lives. No money in the world can buy that satisfaction!

You have that opportunity now before you to be a mentor.

I think of the testimony of Howard Hendricks, a well-known man of God. He was a troubled youth who would have been a write-off in most people's eyes, someone sure to be a failure, a troublemaker, and a kid that was dealt a bad hand. However, a man came into Howard Hendricks' life and became like a father to him and, with patience and determined love, poured into him as well as some other young boys. It changed his life, and now his life is affecting thousands and tens of thousands (possibly more). It was Howard Hendricks who said there should be three people in your life: a Paul, a Barnabas, and a Timothy. These represent (in order): a mentor, a friend who will speak straight to you and encourage you as well, and then lastly someone you are pouring yourself into. So who is your Paul? Who is your Barnabas? Who is your Timothy?

Remember, Brother, everything in the kingdom gives birth to itself. A simple definition of discipleship (and leadership) is found in 1 Corinthians 11:1, "Imitate me, just as I also imitate Christ."

You should be able to say, "Watch how I live my life, imitate how I relate to my wife and how I am a father to my children; watch and imitate me in how I handle my money."

"Watch how I do my business; watch and imitate me in how I relate to people everyday, from the people at the gas station to the restaurant to the one working in the store."

"Watch how I use my free time."

Biblical discipleship is not sitting behind your desk and telling someone a bunch of information and then saying, "Let's do it again tomorrow." No! It is inviting that person into your home; it is teaching on prayer, then modeling it, laying hands on them and getting on your faces together before the Father. It is about going out and doing evangelism and ministry together. It is about applying what we have learned.

Let us return to doing biblical discipleship and seeing disciples who are making disciples of their own. As you may have heard it said, if your "disciple" is not making a disciple, then you do not have a disciple.

Consider the following in God's plan of evangelism. Converts are those that do not reproduce themselves, whereas disciples do. Look at what would happen if you made just four disciples every year, compared to even if you had a convert every day (remember this is through just one person!):

Number of converts vs. number of disciples		
1st year -	365	4
3rd year -	1,095	64
6th year -	2,190	4,096
10th year -	3,650	1,048,576
12th year -	4,380	16,777,216

Are you ready to be imitated? We must imitate Jesus. As we seek Him, we will be conformed to His image more and more, and you will find others wanting to be like you because you look just like Jesus.

Father, we look to Your Son as our only standard and the finisher of our faith; we look to Him as our example. May we present many disciples to You on the final day, who have, in turn, made many more disciples so that we can praise You together around Your glorious throne! We will obey Your command to "go and make disciples," this is Your expectation of each of us, and we will be found faithful to obey. In Jesus Name, we pray.

CHAPTER 21

Elijah, a Man Who Confronted Sin

Then the word of the LORD came to Elijah the
Tishbite, saying, "Arise, go down to meet Ahab
king of Israel, who lives in Samaria. There he is in
the vineyard of Naboth, where he has gone down
to take possession of it. You shall speak to him,
saying, 'Thus says the LORD: Have you murdered
and also taken possession?'" And you shall speak
to him, saying, 'Thus says the LORD: "In the place
where dogs licked the blood of Naboth, dogs shall
lick your blood, even yours."'"

1 Kings 21:17-19

Once a person has committed a sin a single time and then a second time, it appears to him that it is permitted. —A SAYING FROM THE BABYLONIAN TALMUD

We already looked at bringing a consciousness of God's holy presence into the lives of men (Chapter 8) and confronting, specifically, false prophets and heretical teaching (Chapter 13). If we are to walk with God, it will also mean that we have a day-to-day responsibility to be speakers of the truth; we will be used of God to speak His Word, which will bring a revelation of righteousness. His Word reveals sin and the standard of God. One specific example in America of a sin that permeates and needs correction is the continual breaking of the second Commandment, making a god in one's own image. How many say, "My God isn't like that," or "I don't believe that about God." The Word will be like a sword to divide between the soul and spirit and joint and marrow, and judge the thoughts and intentions of the heart (Hebrews 4:12). The Word will speak for itself on Who God really is. There will be true revelation of the **true** God, ...the I AM.

It must be understood, Brother, that you and I dare not confront sin in others (in love and humility) before we have confronted sin in ourselves! Jesus said, "And why do you look at the speck in your brother's eye, but do not consider the plank in your own eye? Or how can you say to your brother, 'Let me remove the speck from your eye;' and look, a plank is in your eye? Hypocrite! First remove the plank from your own eye, and then you will see clearly to remove the speck from your brother's eye" (Matthew 7:3-5).

Jesus wants the planks out and the specks out—out of both sets of eyes! However, you and I must start with our hearts; this is where it always must start—always! Do not go confronting another's sin when your own life is out of order. Before we preach to others, we must preach to ourselves first. We must live the things that we are preaching.

We are to reflect the countenance and character of Jesus, but how does this happen? It happens when we behold His glory and shun the lusts of this world.

I feel led to share a vision that God gave me one time, a

vision that impressed me deeply as an illustration.

In the vision, I was on a road, and there were Christians walking before me on the road. Ahead of us, at the end of the road, was what looked like the sun, shining in its full strength.

It was not the sun, however. For as I looked I could see the outline of a face and a body, and I knew it was Jesus. I could not see the details of His face because of the brightness of His glory. All along the side of the road there was a thick, dark, slimy, brush-like foliage. I looked behind me and saw some other believers. Some were looking ahead, but others were staring into the dark brush, transfixed. It was odd to me that they would look so intently at something that looked so gross; but it made me curious, and so I turned to look.

At first, all I saw were dark, slimy, moss-like bushes. But as I looked, my eyes began to adjust. It was similar to coming inside a house after being out on a bright summer day. At first the room looks dark; but then your eyes begin to adjust, and you see its details around you.

As I continued looking, my eyes adjusted further. I began to see past the slime and nastiness, and I saw the world! I saw people partying and drinking, and women who were dressed seductively. They were calling me to come and join them. They were motioning enticingly with their hands for me to come to them.

It was then I heard the voice of Jesus shout, "Look back at Me!"

Startled, I turned and faced ahead once again. My eyes re-adjusted and I saw the temptation and sin of the world as God saw it—something to be rejected, ugly and leading to death.

The longer we stare at the world, the more we will be enticed, Brother. But, if we fix our eyes on Jesus, we will not be drawn in so easily. We will have His eyes.

How many are staring at the world, looking for the latest fashions; staring into the magazines, books, and movies of the world; being drawn in with the lust of the eyes, the lust of the flesh, and the pride of life?

No more! It is time to live the words we sing, "The cross before me, the world behind me!"

Put before you the cross on which Jesus suffered for your sin, and see sin as He sees it. All we have to do is to think on that blood-stained cross to be reminded of the hatred God has for sin and the terrible penalty that had to be paid with the blood of Jesus Himself. Put the world behind you, for its lusts are passing away; but it is he who does the will of God who will abide forever (1 John 2:17).

Authority to speak to others—true authority—comes when you are living what you are proclaiming. The message must be inseparable from the messenger. I remember my professor of homiletics at Moody Bible Institute, Dr. Dwight Perry, explaining the three requirements for an impactful, dynamic message: logos, pathos, and ethos. These are the Greek terms for word, passion, and ethic or moral character. Someone can give a good word with passion, but if their personal life is not in alignment with the message they preach, you will sense in your spirit that something is not right; there is no real anointing; something is hollow. In the same way, the Word of God must be rightly preached with good moral character and with passion. Without passion, something is missing as well. And obviously it is possible to have passion and moral character but not handle the Word of God rightly. All three aspects must be present for His message to be delivered in the way He desires.

David said in Psalm 139:23-24, "Search me, O God, and

know my heart; try me, and know my anxieties; and see if there is any wicked way in me, and lead me in the way everlasting."

Search me, O God! Make that your prayer now, Brother, in Jesus Name. Now is the time to let the fire come and burn the flesh! Now is the time to lay our lives on the altar!

David said in Psalm 51:6 that God desires "truth in the inward parts." David then says in verses 12 and 13, after his confession and his crying out for a clean heart, "Restore to me the joy of Your salvation, and uphold me by Your generous Spirit. Then I will teach transgressors Your ways, and sinners shall be converted to You" (emphasis mine).

From this moment of deep repentance, from this moment of self-examination (starting with "me" first), comes the authority to teach transgressors God's ways, and to see sinners converted to God! It comes first from the deep revelation of God's holiness, then the experiences of being cleansed by the blood and knowing the joy of God's salvation and deliverance—then bringing that Good News with authority. This is the pattern found in Isaiah 6 in Isaiah's calling.

We can speak with authority to confront sin, but we do not to speak against sin in a condemning way. Rather it is done with the heart to see others restored and reconciled to God. This we know, "But by the grace of God I am what I am" (1 Corinthians 15:10). We must remember, as Paul said in Romans 7, that there is no good thing within us (that is in our flesh). Jesus is your righteousness; now bring others to that revelation. We are to speak in truth, but also in love. It is one thing to preach against sin; it is another thing to have the passionate desire as one preaches, to want to see the sinner restored to right relationship with God.

There is a story that greatly moved me. It was an account from the life of John the apostle (according to Clement of Alexandria's Who is the Rich Man that Shall be Saved? Ch. 42, A.D. 190). John, after seeing a young man converted from a hardened life of crime, discipled him and saw him raised up to become a church leader. After some time, and in the absence of John, this man returned to his sinful ways, even committing murder in his return to a life of banditry. When John heard of this, he sought out the man in a place where robbers, such as this man, were hiding. When the man heard the older Saint John was coming, he fled, with John running after him, calling to him, "Why are you running my son? You still have hope of life." He yelled for him to stop running. Finally, the man stopped, and John embraced the weeping stray. But the man hid the hand he had used to murder behind him. John grabbed it and saw this man restored through his confession and repentance. John, as recorded by Clement, went on to fast repeatedly for this man and begged God with constant prayers to see him grow and be established in the faith. The testimony is that the man went on to become a bishop who would eventually be a martyr for his faith in Christ. O God, give us such a heart as this!

We are responsible to proclaim His righteous Law to the lost; this is to whom the Law is intended for (Timothy 1:9-11). The Law reveals and **brings the knowledge of sin** (Romans 3:20); it then becomes a schoolmaster to bring the lost to Jesus, that they might be justified by faith (Galatians 3:24). By the revelation of God's Law every mouth will be stopped and the entire world will be found guilty before God (Romans 3:19). We can then make known the glorious Gospel of Jesus Christ!

When we have been through the fire and come in contact with His holiness, we will see sin through His eyes. As Evangelist Steve Hill would preach, "Sin is anything Jesus wouldn't do."

Sin needs to be seen for how diabolical it really is. The best and most biblical course I have found regarding the use of the Law in evangelism is <u>The Way of the Master</u> with Ray Comfort and Kirk Cameron. I would encourage anyone and everyone to buy this DVD course series; it has greatly impacted my life and thousands of others. It will equip you to share the Gospel the way Jesus and Paul did (instead of using the popular humanistic method of "Come to Jesus He'll give you peace, love, and joy and He has a wonderful plan for your life.")

However, I state again, true holiness must start with us. I came to a deep revelation of this when I first really started to seek God. Isaiah was, no doubt, an upright, God-fearing man, but when He saw God high and lifted up, he exclaimed, "Woe is me! I am a man of unclean lips, and I dwell in the midst of a people of unclean lips!" (Isaiah 6:5). From this revelation and cleansing came his prayer, "Here I am! Send me."

It was after this revelation of holiness that the Holy Spirit showed me the order of 2 Chronicles 7:14, and I realized it bore witness to my personal experience. 2 Chronicles 7:14 <u>does not</u> say, "If My people who are called by My name will humble themselves, turn from their wicked ways, and pray and seek My face..." No, it says, "If My people who are called by My name will humble themselves, and pray and <u>seek My face</u>, and turn from their wicked ways...."

I found that it is only when we are really seeking God that we even have a right understanding of just how holy He is! And when you seek the face of God, you will also have a revelation of the ugliness of sin and how wicked it really is. Then, you have a choice. Will you turn from it and go forward, or will you stay in that place with God and go no further? This is the context of James 4:8, in saying, "Draw near to God and He will draw near to you." Look again at the verses that follow this promise.

We must, we are commanded to—we cannot afford not to—speak against sin. We must lead others to the understanding that God is holy and that without holiness no one will see Him (Hebrews 12:14). But we must be certain it starts with us; then we will see fruit come forth in others. And we must speak in love, for without love we are just a clanging cymbal and sounding brass.

I have been around men who had little problem in telling others that they were going to hell; they would glory in street preaching. But they lacked a brokenness and the love of God. They could yell, but you would not hear them weep or plead. We must remember: if I "have not love, I am nothing" (1 Corinthians 13:2).

Father, search us and know our hearts. Give us true authority as we walk in truth and in love to proclaim Your standard—uncompromisingly—to prepare everyone for the coming Day of Judgment. In Jesus Name, we pray.

CHAPTER 22

Elijah, a Man Who Was Marked by Turning the Hearts of the Fathers to the Children and the Children to their Fathers

Behold, I will send you Elijah the prophet before the coming of the great and dreadful day of the LORD. And he will turn the hearts of the fathers to the children, and the hearts of the children to their fathers, lest I come and strike the earth with a curse.

Malachi 4:5-6

The words above are the final words of revelation in the Old Testament, the last words before there would be some 400 years of silence.

What does this mean, turning the hearts of the fathers to the children, and the hearts of the children to their fathers?

This is a restoration of family!

Family is the foundation of a culture, the foundation of a civilization, the foundation of a nation. When the family is destroyed, everything will be destroyed. Satan knows this.

The Satanist Aleister Crowley, who admitted to sacrificing hundreds of children, was probably one of the most wicked men who has ever lived. He was used to dictate the "Book of the Law" (which he said came directly from Satan), and he started a Satanic revolution in America and the West. His teachings and writings greatly influenced such people as Jimmy Page from Led Zeppelin; Ozzy Osbourne; Jim Morrison; Timothy Leary; John Lennon and The Beatles; Harry Hay, who led the modern gay movement; Anton LaVey, the co-founder of the church of Satan; The Rolling Stones; Charles Manson; Sting; David Bowie; and Scientology founder L. Ron Hubbard.

He wanted to raise up a youth culture and to further break the relationship between fathers and their children.

Do you know what Crowley said was the number one enemy for his followers to fight against? The family! He said, "Think what horrid images it evokes from the mind. Not only Victorian; wherever the family has been strong it has always been an engine of tyranny.... Curse them! They are always in the way...to the performance of this work (the New Age) the nearest obstacle and the most obvious is the family." (DVD series "They Sold Their Souls to Rock n Roll", volume 2). There are a lot of things he could have said, but he said the number one enemy was the family. That is why he pushed so hard in favor of fornication, sexual immorality, homosexuality, and so forth—to see the family destroyed.

I remember the testimony of a speaker at a Promise Keepers event back in the early '90s. He was traveling on an airplane, and as the stewardess brought the meal, the man sitting next to him denied the food. It provoked this brother in Christ to ask the man why he was not eating. The man simply replied, "I'm fasting." The brother thought perhaps he was a believer, but when he asked him what he was fasting about, he replied, "I'm from the church of Satan, and I'm fasting for the destruction of Christian families."

Hello!?! There is a war, Brother! It is time to rise up and fast for the restoration of Christian families!

How else has the enemy been at work? We have already seen the effects of the latchkey generation, and it continues—parents just working and working and working. For what? What you have is not enough? You are going to work more hours and forfeit time with your kids? So, now, instead of the fathers teaching the children, the world is teaching the children. Come on, Brother, let us not deceive ourselves. How much influence do you think a man has on his kids when he spends on average ten minutes or less a day with them, and most kids are spending hours a day exposed to friends who come from homes where there is anything but the presence of Christ, where they sit in front of the television for hours, read books that glorify what God hates, where they are taught humanism and evolution in public school, where they listen for hours to the trash music of this world (I am amazed at what Christian parents allow their kids to listen to that is filled with violence, the vilest sexually immoral lyrics, and constant vulgarity), and where they surf the Internet for hours, being exposed to pornography and all kinds of images of lust and vain glory. Who is raising your kids, Brother? You or the world? Crowley said, "Let me seduce the boys...and the oldsters may totter unconverted to their graves. Then, these boys become men, and may bring about the new Heaven and the new Earth...but without an army I am useless...give me my army, young men; and we will sweep these dogs into the sea." (A. Crowley, The World's Tragedy, 1985, p. 25)

The spirit of Elijah is going to come against this in the name of Jesus. We are going to be used to see families walking together in love, unity, power and truth! How is this going to happen? I believe that when the sons see conviction in their fathers, when they see that their fathers are not living shallow, compromised lives, but lives full of vision and passion and divine love, they will follow. Youth are drawn towards passion, to conviction, to fire. It is time they see it in the men of the church.

It is in the heart of children to be like their fathers. God put that there!

When the fathers run with passion for the glory of God, the sons will say, "I want to be like my dad." So many sons have such pride in their fathers who go off to war. Why? Because it resonates to the son, "My dad believes in something so strongly, he is willing to die for it." That should be the testimony of our children for us in our walk with Jesus. "My dad has given himself completely to the glory of God; he has died to himself and lives to advance the Kingdom of God. He is a man who wars in the Spirit, a man of the deepest convictions. He is willing to die for what he believes in."

When they see that they are going to say, "I want to be like my dad."

Too often instead of fathers giving their blessing to their child, they have cursed their children with words like, "You're always like this," or "You're always doing that!" or "You'll never...." Just curses.

The Bible says that we are priests of the Lord (1 Peter 2:9), and one of the responsibilities of the priest is to bless! Brothers, it is time to bless your children, to declare over them words like, "You're going to glorify God in your life. You're going to walk with God, know His love, and experience His glory! You're not going to listen to the voice of the world, but you're going to know the voice of your heavenly Father! I bless you with a heart of worship like David; I bless you to have visions like Isaiah; I bless you to have determination like Ezekiel; I bless you to walk with God like Enoch; I bless you to have favor like Daniel and Joseph; I bless you with a broken heart of intercession like Jeremiah. I bless you with wisdom like Solomon; I bless you to be bold like the apostles; and I bless you with a heart for the church and the lost like your Lord Jesus Christ! You're going to be a young man or woman of the Word of God!"

But, Brothers, we must not stop there. We have a mandate from God to bless a fatherless generation—to bless them in Jesus name, to declare life over them, to declare hope over them, to declare that God's will be done in their lives. Look at the verse again... "to turn the hearts of the fathers to **the** children, and the hearts of the children to their fathers." It doesn't say "their" children, but "the" children. God wants to use the fathers in the church to bless their own children **and** to bless the children who are not biologically theirs. God is going to use you to lay hands and bless children who have been neglected or rejected, so that they are not another "dead fish" being swept down the filthy river of this world, but to be alive in Christ, to swim against the current, and to bring change! In Jesus Name!

As I spent time doing inner-city ministry, working with so many of the fatherless, I was so broken. I asked God for His wisdom; I asked, "What can be done?" I remember that God told me to study the book of Proverbs. I felt led to prepare a document in which I organized the book of Proverbs into categories. The Lord, I believe, told me that Proverbs is given specifically for the sons (in fact the term "my son" actually appears some 23 times), to be their wisdom in what should be taught by the father. So, I used that book as my manual. (If you would like a copy, I would be happy to email it to you at wadeandkate@gmail.com.) So many of these boys do not know how to be men. I thought of the Jewish culture and so many other cultures in the world where there is some kind of rite of passage. And so, we had one for our inner-city boys, too. We basically took eight boys with seven men of God, who would be by their side for three days, leading them through each day, showing them how to be a young man of discipline (from personal hygiene to their personal time with God), doing physical challenges together, having fun together, and exhorting them in the Word of God. (See the Appendix B for more detail). Then, to have the privilege of laying hands on them and declaring the blessing of God over their lives! We gave them a token, a necklace depicting the "shield of faith" with Joshua 1:9 on the back. It greatly affected those boys.

That is just a beginning. There needs to be discipleship and an ongoing relationship. They need to see that we want to invest in their lives because we really do care for them and love them. Brothers, we need to reclaim this generation that is basically fatherless. If we do not take this seriously, be assured that the enemy will. The Elijah generation will be used to turn the kids' hearts back to the fathers and ultimately back to their heavenly Father. HalleluYah! Let us go and be the restorers of streets to dwell in (Isaiah 58:12). God's heart is burning for the fatherless; ours should be as well.

Father, give us Your heart! We want the Father's heart! We

need the Father's heart! Let our lives reflect our Father who is in heaven! We ask this in faith, in Jesus Name!

CHAPTER 23

John, a Man Who Prepared the Coming of Jesus (the Message of Repentance in Light of His Imminent Return)

In those days John the Baptist came preaching in the wilderness of Judea, and saying, "Repent, for the kingdom of heaven is at hand!" For this is he who was spoken of by the prophet Isaiah, saying: "The voice of one crying in the wilderness: 'Prepare the way of the LORD; make His paths straight.'"

Matthew 3:1-3

Just as the closing words of Malachi—which led into 400 years of prophetic silence—left a deep impression, so will the first prophetic words breaking that silence also be of profound significance. John the Baptist comes onto the scene, and what is his cry? "Prepare the way of the Lord; make His paths straight!" Silence, and now the earnest expectation that we are at the end, the fulfillment of Scripture—the Messiah is coming! There was an urgency in his voice, he was a passionate alarm call resounding in the land. Just like a boss that steps in to see how his workers are performing, or a coach that walks in on a practice, or a father in on his children when he's told them what he expects. There is a sudden self examination, "Am I doing what he told me to do? Will he be pleased? Did I meet his expectations?" John was saying wake up and get ready, for the King is coming!

And He came! Praise You LORD! Just as it was prophesied.

Jesus rebuked the Pharisees for knowing the seasons, but not discerning the time of His first coming (Matthew 16:1-3). What do you think He will expect of us, when there are more then twice as many prophecies concerning His second coming? Be ready! This is His message.

Have you ever studied the New Testament's perspective of time? Consider what you prayerfully read below...

Jesus' words that the disciples will not have gone through all the cities of Israel before the Son of Man comes (Matthew 10).

The parable of those bidden to the wedding feast. They were told that everything was ready, but they used the affairs of this life as excuses for not coming (Matthew 22:1-5).

Jesus' warning that if the owner of the house had known at what hour the thief would come, he would not have allowed his house to be broken into (Matthew 24:43).

Jesus' parable of the 10 virgins, which speaks of the importance of alertness and of His coming at any hour (Matthew 25:1-13).

Jesus' message of entrusting the work to his servants and their being ready for his return, "lest coming suddenly he find [them] sleeping. And what I say to you, I say to all, Watch!" (Mark 13:32-37).

Jesus' parable of the rich man who thought he had much time to relax and take it easy but whose soul was required of him that night (Luke 12:16-21).

Jesus' warning to be like men who are waiting for their master to return from a wedding, so that "when he comes and knocks, they may open unto Him immediately" (Luke 12:35-40).

Jesus' warning to those who will be punished for not preparing themselves and will be "beaten" (Luke 12:42-48).

The command to be alert and pray to escape the things that are coming and to stand before Jesus (Luke 21:36).

The understanding that these were the last days by the sign of the Holy Spirit being poured out on all flesh (Acts 2:43-45).

The way the apostles lived, giving themselves continually to prayer and to the ministry of the word (Acts 6:3-4).

The lifestyle of Paul, who testified of working tirelessly with urgency and said, "Therefore watch, and remember that for three years I did not cease to warn everyone night and day with tears" (Acts 20:31).

Paul's exhortation to not "sleep" now that "our salvation is nearer than when we first believed" (Romans 13:11).

Paul did not want the Corinthians coming up short in any gift as they waited for the coming of the Lord (1 Corinthians 1:7-8).

Paul told us that "the time is short" and that people should live in light of that urgency in all areas of their lives (1 Corinthians 7:29-31).

The constant reminder, by way of the Lord's Supper, that as

often as you and I partake, we "proclaim the Lord's death till He comes" (1 Corinthians 11:26).

We are commanded to walk in wisdom and redeem the time (Ephesians 5:16).

We are given a command, "Let your gentleness be known to all men. The Lord is at hand" (Philippians 4:5).

The day will come like a thief in the night (1 Thessalonians 5:2).

The church of Thessalonica was so expecting the coming of Jesus that they needed to be rebuked because they stopped working! (1 Thessalonians 5).

There is a crown of righteousness promised to those who love His appearing, those who live in light of the imminence of His return (2 Timothy 4:8).

We are to look for the glorious appearance of Jesus (Titus 2:12-13).

We are not to forsake the assembling of ourselves, but to exhort one another, more and more. Why? More and more "as [we] see the Day approaching" (Hebrews 10:25).

We are told to have patience, so that we may receive the promise of God, "and He who is coming will come and will not tarry" (Hebrews 10:35-37).

The examples of faith were said to see themselves as "strangers and pilgrims on the earth" (Hebrews 11:13).

The rich are reminded, "no sooner has the sun risen with a burning heat then it withers the grass; its flower falls, and its beautiful appearance perishes. So the rich man also will fade away in his pursuits" (James 1:9-11).

James warns those who speak confidently that they will go to such and such a city to buy and sell. He says, "You do not know what will happen tomorrow. For what is your life? It is even a vapor that appears for a little time and then vanishes away. Instead you ought to say, If the Lord wills, we shall live and do this or that" (James 4:13-15).

James says again, "be patient" because "the coming of the Lord is at hand" (James 5:7-8).

And he tells us again not to have a grudge against each other because "the Judge is standing at the door!" (James 5:9).

Peter talks about looking forward to the revelation of Jesus Christ in the context of suffering and persecution (1 Peter 1:6-7).

Peter talks about flesh being like grass and the glory of man like a flower that is soon withered (1 Peter 1:24).

Peter says, "The end of all things is at hand; therefore be serious and watchful in your prayers" (1 Peter 4:7).

Peter talks about the mockers, who scoff and say, "Where is the promise of His coming?" But about this they are willingly ignorant; God is patient wanting more to repent before it is too late. Peter reminds us that we are to hasten the coming of the Lord's coming (2 Peter 3:3-15).

John said that it is "the last hour," and that even now there are many antichrists in the world (1 John 2:17-19).

John told believers to be ready at His coming lest they be ashamed of Him. (He would not be giving the warning if it were not possible, i.e., some will be ashamed) (1 John 2:28).

Jude reveals that even Enoch sensed the urgency of the Lord's coming (with ten thousand of His saints) and bringing His judgment against the ungodly (Jude 14-15).

The Book of Revelation introduces itself as, "the revelation of Jesus Christ, which God gave Him to show His servants—things which must shortly take place" (Revelation 1:1).

The promise is: "Blessed is he who reads and those who hear the words of this prophecy, and keep those things which are written in it; for the time is near" (Revelation 1:3).

And finally, Jesus closes the canon of Scripture by declaring three times, "Behold, I am coming quickly" (Revelation 22:11-21).

What is the message? Your life and my life are but a breath, and Jesus is coming soon. Either way, be ready! How much clearer can it get? This is the way we are to live,… prepared! Live your life in such a way that today you are ready to meet with Jesus and give an account of your life.

Let us heed the words that Moses, the man of God, used in summarizing the brevity of his life, "Teach us to number our days, that we may gain a heart of wisdom" (Psalm 90:12). I had made this a prayer for years in my life, and I can bear witness that God has answered. Many have said that I have been allowed to see much happen in a short period time, but I know it is God honoring His Word, for I am continually reminded of my mortality and am asking God to maximize the time, this very brief time, I have on the earth. So many squander their time and act as if there is no eternal ramification. What you and I do with this short time on earth will have eternal consequences. We want our memories to be filled with visions of His glory, manifestations of His Kingdom, revelations from the Holy Spirit, and souls coming to Jesus. Yes, we will have memories of times with friends and family, but we must seek to align our lives with what will bring glory to God and eternal reward. Look again at the vision, passion, and commitment of Paul in 1 Corinthians 9:16-27 for an example. Look at the urgency in Paul's tone and the words He uses: "woe is me," "servant to all," "win the more," "by all means save some," "run in such a way that you obtain it," "fight," "discipline," "subjection." Or read again

Philippians 3, where Paul considers all else loss, (or rubbish) for the sake of the knowledge of Christ. One short life—what are we going to do with it? We are standing on a huge graveyard; billions have died, and here we are, alive in this moment of time. This is our opportunity; what will we do with the life given to us by God? By God's grace, Brother, live in such a way that you have no regrets when you are looking at your final moments on earth.

If you knew that Jesus was coming in 10 days, how would you live your life? That is how you are to live now, my Brother. John Wesley was asked how would he live his life differently if he knew he were to die that night. He said that, basically, he would live the same way he had—no regrets! He would not suddenly change his life style because Jesus was coming; he had a peace that what he was doing was in the will of God. We should be living the same way.

Let us live wisely! Be ready, be prepared, and prepare others: your family, the Church, and those who need Jesus. Do not put it off! "Set your house in order," Brother! (see 2 Kings 20:1).

Father, prepare us for this coming Day! We do not want to be living in self-deception. Let us walk in the revelation of Your Word and be ready; let us be found watching (with our lamps burning) and prepared for Your return. We do not want any regrets, Father. Help us to live in light of eternity, teach us to number our days that we may gain a heart of wisdom, we ask, in Jesus' Name.

CHAPTER 24

John and Elijah, Men Who Showed They Were Not Attached to This World's Wealth

Now John himself was clothed in camel's hair, with a leather belt around his waist; and his food was locusts and wild honey.

Matthew 3:4

So they answered him, "A hairy man wearing a leather belt around his waist." And he said, "It is Elijah the Tishbite."

2 Kings 1:8

To hunger and thirst after righteousness is when nothing in the world can fascinate us so much as being near to God.... You cannot buy or wear or sell except that which is pleasing to the

Lord. Jesus becomes Lord over your wants and desires. You love that which God loves and hate that which God hates.... If you can be fascinated by anything else in the world, you don't have what God wants you to have." – Smith Wigglesworth – (W.Hacking, "Smith Wigglesworth Remembered", Harrison House, 1981, pp.78, 101, 83)

John did not come with long flowing robes or in the wealth of the world. He did not come on a nice horse or with an entourage of servants or bodyguards. He did not say, "Go tell the people of my great ministry; tell them to send money to us; tell them to give their seed offering; they will reap great riches."

No! John revealed where his heart was. It was not for things of this world. He was storing up treasures in heaven!

For too long a wrong message has been communicated in the church. But the world is not stupid. Most know the story of Jesus; they know how He came. They ask, "How is it that Jesus came in such a humble, simple way, but you seem to be so opposite to this?" They are asking good questions. For too long it has not been recognized that our hearts are not on the world to come, but on this world. Jesus said, "Where your treasure is, there will your heart be also." Jesus spoke more about money, wealth, and possessions than any other subject, and he said you **cannot** serve two masters.

Everyone should see that we are not living for this world and our lives should demonstrate, like John, we truly are storing up treasure in heaven. I am not suggesting that we go out and start dressing in camel's hair and a leather belt and eating locusts. However, there should be a clear testimony in our lives of where our citizenship is and what we are investing the most in (which openly demonstrates where our heart is). **Our lives should be marked by sacrificial giving**. Let us give generously—hilariously— to the work of God and to those who are really hurting. I am sure you are fully aware of the statistics indicating that most Christians give perhaps two percent of their income. Ten percent should be the minimum. That was under the Law, but we are under grace, which should encourage us to give more. Jesus' expectation was for us to give more now that we are empowered and led by His Spirit.

We can learn something from our Mennonite brothers. I have a good friend, Patrick, who grew up as a Mennonite and he exemplifies this attribute of the Elijah generation beautifully to me. He lives simply and gives generously. Everything in his home has spiritual significance to him, and he sees it as an instrument of spiritual warfare. Everything he owns has a testimony of some kind; there is no room for excess, just for what God has given him (mostly through others). He truly lives the reality of it being "more blessed to give than to receive" (Acts 20:35).

Where should that money go? To the advancement of the kingdom of God. I hear the stories, (in Guinea Bissau and America), of big churches who are sending so few, or people being sent out by the church without being adequately supported in the basic things. How many missionaries is your church supporting? Are you supporting a missionary or some kind of Gospel ministry among the unreached? How much of your money are you investing in the kingdom of God? Do you think that God entrusted all that money to you so that you could spend it on yourselves or to give just a small sum to His work? Or to continually make the church building more aesthetically appealing and comfortable?

The promise of God is 2 Corinthians 9:8, "And God is able to make all grace abound toward you, that you, always having all sufficiency in all things, may have an abundance for every good work."

The emphasis of the Word of God is to give, not to receive!

Much of the church has lost its vision. God wants you to model something quite different: to live and speak the message of Paul to Timothy in 1 Timothy 6:5-10:

"Now godliness with contentment is great gain. For we brought nothing into this world, and it is certain we can carry nothing out. And having food and clothing, with these we shall be content. But those who desire to be rich fall into temptation and a snare, and into many foolish and harmful lusts which drown men in destruction and perdition. For the love of money is a root of all kinds of evil for which some have strayed from the faith in their greediness, and pierced themselves through with many sorrows."

You do not want your money to be a testimony against you on the Day of Judgment, bearing witness of your "earthliness" rather than your "heavenliness." Is it not interesting that the seriousness of God's judgment in Acts 5 is connected to money/possessions? We really need to take heed. If the church is mobilized in giving, we can see whole nations bombarded with the Gospel by way of sent missionaries, well-supported national missionaries, the distribution of Bibles and Christian literature, radio ministry, and so forth — whole nations! What would happen if schools of discipleship were to be raised up in major cities all over to train national believers? It could impact the nation if those schools are in the fire of the Holy Spirit, giving solid biblical teaching and creating biblical community.

Where does most of the money in America go, however? Too many times it goes to fulfill one's own desires: over-priced coffee, entertainment, clothes, and possessions and the upkeep of our palaces! We need to remember that all we have belongs to God; we are stewards. God is good, but that does not negate the need for stewardship and the understanding that we will be held accountable.

"He who is faithful in what is least is faithful also in much; and he who is unjust in what is least is unjust also in much. Therefore if you have not been faithful in the unrighteous mammon, who will commit to your trust the true riches?" (Luke 16:10-11).

It is time again to ask the Holy Spirit what He thinks about what we are doing with what belongs to Him. If we say that Jesus is our Lord, He is Lord of our money as well.

If we get the vision of God, we are going to see many laborers raised up, funded, and sent out into God's vineyard to harvest souls for His glory. It will also be a powerful testimony to a world that has grown skeptical of Christians and their lifestyle. I believe that the church will really gain the ear of the world when we take ownership of the poor, the needy, and the downtrodden rather than leaving that work to the government. The church can do these things better because the church brings not just finances but also the culture of the kingdom of God, the power of the Holy Spirit, the love of Christ, and the words of God to bring lasting inner change. This change does not just affect the way someone lives materially; it is a change of the heart, vision and life.

Brother, be an example. If someone wanted to see how you spend your money, you should be able to show him your checking account history with no cause for hesitation or shame. People will see that you are not living for the things of this world; they will understand that you are investing your money in what you are preaching. May God see on that great day that you have invested well in His Kingdom and that your heart was for the lost and for those who are suffering and hungry.

Elijah and John shunned the wealth of this world, and that gave them an authority. They did not need wealth to talk to the wealthy; they did not need to dress a certain way in order to reach leaders. They just needed the anointing of God. Do not believe the lie that your witness will be affected if you do not have what others have or that somehow your money is a platform for you. The only platform you need is the one God gives to a life that is completely surrendered to His Spirit.

We must shun consumerism. What does your budget look like? What do most church budgets look like? Where are hundreds and thousands of dollars going? Do you even know? You have a responsibility to know. There are millions of people going to hell. Let us put our money where God wants it.

"Riches do not profit in the day of wrath, but righteousness delivers from death" (Proverbs 11:4).

"He who trusts in his riches will fall, but the righteous will flourish like foliage" (Proverbs 11:28).

"There is one that makes himself rich, yet has nothing; and one who makes himself poor, yet has great riches" (Proverbs 13:7).

"He who is greedy for gain troubles his own house, but he who hates bribes will live" (Proverbs 15:27).

"Whoever shuts his ears to the cry of the poor will also cry himself and not be heard" (Proverbs 21:13).

"[The lazy man] covets greedily all day long, but the righteous gives and spares not" (Proverbs 21:26).

"He who has a generous eye will be blessed, for he gives of his bread to the poor" (Proverbs 22:9).

"One who increases his possessions by usury and extortion gathers it for him who will pity the poor" (Proverbs 28:8).

"He who gives to the poor will not lack, but he who hides his eyes will have many curses" (Proverbs 28:27).

"He who loves silver will not be satisfied with silver, nor

he who loves abundance, with increase. This also is vanity. When goods increase, they increase who eat them; so what profit have the owners, except to see them with their eyes? The sleep of a laboring man is sweet, whether he eats little or much; but the abundance of the rich will not permit him to sleep" (Ecclesiastes 5:10-12).

Father, we repent on behalf of the church for not reflecting the kingdom of heaven, but so often reflecting the kingdom of this world. We repent of the love of money in the church. O God, forgive us as a church for misrepresenting You and bringing reproach to Your name with allowing the world to see in us the love of money and the storing up of treasure on earth, instead of in heaven! Use us to model what John and Elijah demonstrated, and may the world see that our citizenship is truly in heaven. In Jesus' Name, we pray.

Week #4
Discussion questions and points of application

1. Have you been persecuted in any way? How did you respond? How did it strengthen your faith?

2. Ask the Father to show you who you are to be discipling. Ask Him even for a specific number of disciples for this coming 6 months. If you want a basic format on how to lead someone in discipleship feel free to email me at wadeandkate@gmail.com and I will send you discipleship material.

3. Are you living in way that today could be your last, and you are ready to give an account of your life? We have

no promise of tomorrow, we have today to be obedient. Have a time of prayer of consecration to God as a group. If you are not familiar with "The Way of the Master" evangelism course, make it a priority to do it as a group.

4. Write out a specific blessing you want to speak over your wife (or future wife whether you know her yet or not). Write out a specific blessing to speak over your children and/ or over a child who doesn't have a father's blessing yet. Then go and speak it over their lives in Jesus Name.

5. Pray together as a group the prayer of Moses in Psalm 90:12. Discuss what are some practical truths of what a life looks like that is living in light of eternity, that has things in order. Then write down what you believe the Spirit is revealing to you personally in what He wants you to do, which makes the way you live your life make sense in light of eternity.

6. Time to get real! Ask the Holy Spirit to reveal to each other in prayer how He wants the money that God sends to you to be spent. Ask Him if there is a certain organization or person that He wants you to support for the advancement of God's Kingdom. Perhaps He is asking you to start something. Maybe He will reveal a ministry He wants you to do and to invest your money in to reach souls for Jesus. Ask and you will receive, seek and you will find, knock and it will be opened to you.

CHAPTER 25

John, a Man Who Openly Rebuked the Spirit of Religion (Spiritual Pride/ Self-Righteousness)

But when he saw many of the Pharisees and Sadducees come to his baptism, he said to them, "Brood of vipers! Who warned you to flee from the wrath to come? Therefore bear fruits worthy of repentance."

Matthew 3:7-8

Religion (in the sense of following rules, apart from having a relationship with God) has damned a lot of people to hell. It has an outward appearance of righteousness, but inwardly, the heart is **not** right. It has turned many people away from God and His Son. A lot of people have not seen Jesus; instead they have seen rules. And they were not brought into contact with Jesus; they only heard about Him. Religion has a form of godliness but denying the power of it (1 Timothy 4:2). Jesus warns against the spirit of religion—the leaven of the Pharisees, which is hypocrisy (Luke 12).

Hypocrisy – the practice of claiming to have moral standards or beliefs to which one's own behavior does not conform; pretense. From the Greek hupokrisis 'acting of a theatrical part' from 'hupokrinesthai 'play a part, pretend'(The New Oxford American Dictionary).

Jesus was very articulate about those characteristics when He rebuked the Pharisees. Matthew 23 reveals a lot about those who have a religious spirit:

1. They do not practice what they preach (but they sure do like to preach and show others just how much they know!) (v.3).

2. They put heavy burdens on others that they themselves are not willing to carry (v.4), including rules outside of the Word of God (Matthew 15:9).

3. What they do, they do to be seen by men (v.5).

4. They "wear" their "devotion" for others to take notice (v.5).

5. They love the place of honor at important social events (v.6).

6. They love the seat of honor at religious services and events (v.6).

7. They love to be seen as popular and well-liked. They love to be acknowledged (v.7).

8. They love to be called some respectable title (and many times will insist that you call them by that title) (v.7). It should also be said here that they look for the credentials of men to verify one's authority to do the work of God (Mark 11:28, Acts 4:7).

9. They inhibit men from entering the Kingdom of God rather than helping them enter (v.13).

10. Their fruit can be seen in the lives of their converts and disciples (v.15). (Like produces like; the tree is known by its fruit.)

11. They lack spiritual discernment and draw attention to the physical rather than the spiritual; they are more likely to reverence a place or object than the act of worship and the presence of God (v.16-22).

12. They draw attention to the fine details of religious duty and neglect the more important issues—justice, mercy, and faith (v.23).

13. They are motivated, not by the love of God, but by greed, money, personal gain, and gratifying their personal desires and pleasure (v.25).

14. They bring more attention to their outward appearance before men than they do to the condition of their hearts (which are full of hypocrisy and sinful desires) before God (v.26-28).

15. They love to honor men and women of the past. However, had they lived in the time of those men and women of the past, they would have persecuted them

in the same way they persecute and resist the things of the Spirit before them presently (v.29-32). They resist the power and miracles of the Holy Spirit and want to remain in control, and they fight against those who have the anointing of God. When the religious see their own "disciples" leaving to go to one who is truly anointed by God, they become enraged (as seen in Acts 4 and 7).

The clearest sign of the Pharisee is the lack of love. John was clear that it is love that marks whether someone really knows God or not (1 John 4). These who come in a spirit of religion bring reproach to the testimony of Jesus, because they claim to be of Jesus, but Jesus said that it would be love for one another whereby others would know who His disciples are (John 13:34-35).

One way this spirit of religion needs to be rebuked is the same way Jesus did it; they need to be reminded that the measure with which they judge others, they will stand before God and be judged by the same measure (Matthew 7:2). They need to be reminded that, it is the merciful who are blessed (literally "happy") and who will receive mercy, and they need to be reminded that "there is nothing covered that will not be revealed, nor hidden that will not be known. Therefore whatever you have spoken in the dark will be heard in the light, and what has been spoken in the ear in inner rooms will be proclaimed on the housetops" (Luke 12:2-3).

We must now show those who have been wounded by this spirit of religion the true Jesus, and that He can heal them of these wounds. We need to explain to them that others have come falsely representing Jesus. Then, we are to lead them into the presence of Jesus through empathetic prayer and by releasing blessings over them in place of the curses.

God wants to see any who are gripped in this religious attitude repent; He has no pleasure in the death of the wicked (Ezekiel 18:23). He wants them to confess their sin and humble themselves, for them to pray out, "I was wrong. I did not exalt Jesus; I exalted myself. I talked about Jesus, but I did not live like Jesus. I have put great burdens on people shoulders, but I should have come alongside them to help them. I did not come in the way Jesus came. I did not come with the heart of a servant. I did not come with a heart that says, "I prefer others above myself." I did not demonstrate the fulfillment of the Law, which is to love the Lord with all my heart, soul, mind, and strength and love my neighbor as myself."

If someone has been gripped in this attitude or has grown up surrounded by such an environment, he needs to have his mind renewed with the Word of God, and I would suggest he give himself to meditating on scriptures about love. Probably the most excellent series of messages I personally have heard on love is David Harwood's The Love of God Project (www.loveofgodproject.com). I would encourage anyone to listen to it; it will deeply impact you.

Love will conquer this spirit of religion. They must learn the culture of the Kingdom of God, which is opposite to the culture of this world. If you want to be first, you have to be last. If you want to be the leader, you need to be the servant. If you want to be seen by God, you have to act in secret. If you want to live, you need to die to yourself and your desires. The culture of the Kingdom of God says that it is what is inside that matters—your thought life. It says to love, to bless, to do good, and to pray for those who oppose you.

May the men of God arise and come against the religious spirit, and model for others (first to their families) the culture of the Kingdom of God. For where there is love, there is no fear (1 John

4:18) and there will be true unity (Colossians 3:14).

I know a man of God who was a leader over missionaries in a large denomination for the region of West Africa. He prayed 1 Corinthians 13:1-8 into his life every day—every day. It was little wonder to me that God used him and lifted him up to a place of leadership. God honored the man's prayer; he exemplified love, he fulfilled the Law, and he helped counter that spirit of religion that would rear its ugly head at times. May we do the same and be marked by what Jesus said would reveal that we are truly His disciples.

The Elijah generation will rebuke the spirit of religion, because true love warns, and an open rebuke is better than hidden love (Proverbs 27:5).

Father, give us courage to rebuke in love, the spirit of religion and to trust the results to Your hands. Help us to bring Your healing to those affected by the spirit of religion, in Jesus' Name.

CHAPTER 26

Elijah and John, Men Who Preached of the Coming Judgment and the Need for Deep Self-Examination of the Fruit of One's Life

And even now the ax is laid to the root of the trees. Therefore every tree which does not bear good fruit is cut down and thrown into the fire. I indeed baptize you with water unto repentance, but He who is coming after me is mightier than I, whose sandals I am not worthy to carry. He will baptize you with the Holy Spirit and fire. His winnowing fan is in His hand, and He will thoroughly clean out His threshing floor, and gather His wheat into the barn; but He will burn up the chaff with unquenchable fire.

Matthew 3:10-12

"The Christian is called to proclaim and prosecute an irreconcilable war against his bosom sins; those sins which have lain nearest his heart, must now be trampled under his feet." — William Gurnall

John calls attention to <u>what kind</u> of fruit is coming forth from one's life (good or bad).

However, Jesus reveals <u>where</u> good fruit comes from and what our focus is to be on, that is, abiding in Him (John 15).

When I lived in Dakar, Senegal, where my family and I served for two years, I came face to face with Islam. It was an oppressive environment. It was the wake-up call many missionaries get; most of these people are not just waiting for you to come tell them about Jesus (In fact, many do not want you to be there!). I remember how I did all I could to be Jesus and preach Jesus, but I saw no fruit. I struggled and struggled. Finally, as our furlough was approaching, I was thinking about returning to America and facing those who were praying and supporting and looking for the miracle stories and the conversions. I think you know what I am talking about. Americans are pragmatic, and they want results. If they are not getting them, they can quickly move on or say (maybe not say it all the time but think it), "What's the problem? You need to figure out what the issue is and fix it."

I had been praying, but I came to the end of myself and asked God to help me in that dark city and country. I asked why I had not seen anything significant happen (in my eyes, anyway). Then, God gave me a dream. In it, I was back in America, standing before my home church and about to preach, but I had nothing to say! It was an agonizing and awkward feeling (as you can imagine) to have all eyes on me and to have absolutely <u>nothing</u> to say. That was it, the end of the dream. A few days later, I had another dream; I was in the same situation with the same problem: nothing to say. I awoke and asked God, "Please help me to understand." A few days later, I had the same dream again. This time at least the Bible was open, but I still had nothing to say! After this dream I was broken hearted, for obviously I just was not getting the message. I asked God for mercy, asked Him to help me understand, and told Him that I was listening. A few days later, I had a fourth dream. The scene was the same; I was asked to preach, but this time, as I stood up, the Bible was open and I could see what it was opened to—John 15. I think you will believe me when I say, when I woke up I studied that passage! The Lord spoke to me and told me to stop focusing on the fruit, but to focus on abiding in Him. He said the fruit will naturally come from the abiding. It will be there; it will manifest on its own, but I must focus on abiding in Him.

So, I prayed for Him to help me to abide, and He did. Interestingly, it was not but perhaps two weeks later that God gave me something to write home about! The fruit came. Here I was in a Muslim neighborhood and now one night at about half past ten, screams came from our neighbor's house. It sounded like a woman giving birth. I went out onto our roof, a flat roof on which you could walk out, and looked down and saw a young lady (who was not pregnant). She was rolling around on the floor with her family surrounding her. They were throwing water on her face and slapping her, trying to get her out of the state she was in. The Spirit immediately confirmed in my heart that which you might have already guessed, that this was demonic. I actually made excuses as to why I should not go down ("Look, Lord, the door is closed, its late, the shutters are shut..."), but the Lord said, "Go down."

When I knocked on the door, the woman of the house

immediately opened the door. Without even asking any questions, she led me straight back to where this young lady was. I found out later that this fifteen year old girl had suffered these demonic attacks on and off for three years. They had taken her to the hospital and given her medication, but nothing helped her. When I came to her, her eyes were rolled back in her head; just the whites of her eyes were showing. Her body was contorted, saliva was around her mouth, and her nose was completely crusted over with a layer of mucus. The family looked at me helplessly. I knelt down beside her and the Spirit instantly brought to my mind Mark 16, "These signs will follow those who believe: In My name they will cast out demons." As I commanded the demons to leave her in Jesus' Name, there was a moment of stillness, and then she sat up, looking around with her expression seeming to say, "Where am I?" She went over and washed her face as her family stood there in shock. I told them I would be back the next day. I came back, and she surrendered to Jesus and suffered no more attacks. HalleluYah!

When you abide in Jesus, He will lead you; He will (literally) open doors no man can shut (Revelation 3:8)! He will make his guidance so obvious; you will find yourself at times simply being carried along by the power of the Spirit. Just fix your attention on abiding in Christ!

I saw other "fruit" from that trip before coming back home. I believe that that neighborhood knew that the Kingdom of God had come!

We must focus on abiding in Christ, and from that will flow the fruit that God expects. We will do the works He has predestined us to walk in (Ephesians 2:10, Philippians 2:13).

The Spirit in John also brings a deep sobriety to those who had ears to hear and causes them to examine their lives.

Paul commands, "Examine yourselves as to whether you are in the faith" (2 Corinthians 13:5). The Elijah generation will bring a deeper understanding of this self-examination and the reality, gravity, and nearness of the Day of Judgment. This is going to be a serious, somber day, yet it is amazing how few preach about it. John the Baptist talked about it; Jesus talked about it; and so did Paul.

How many sermons have you heard on Luke 12:45-48? Have you heard even one in your life?

There is a time to laugh, and there is a time to be serious. It seems we have swung the pendulum to the former in some circles of the Church and that if you talk of serious things, you are just viewed as morbid or not filled with the Spirit. Some may conclude that you know nothing of the "new wine." What would they have thought of the prophets of old? I would have to believe that such churches spend little time (or no time) in the book of Revelation. Picture that day in your mind. Is there anything to laugh at? Is that a day to take lightly? He is our Father, but He is God. We have to be careful to not cross the line of relating to God by our own conception of the word "Father," at the expense of His being Almighty God, Creator of Heaven and Earth, whose primary attribute declared by the angels is "Holy!". It is not "Love." The picture of heaven is not cuddling on God's lap. Read it for yourself, in Revelation 7:9-17. We will be dressed in white around the throne of God, declaring His worthiness. He is love, but we must remember He is the Eternal One. He is not totally like us; He alone is the Great I AM. It was the apostle John who leaned on Jesus' chest, but in Revelation he sees the glorified Jesus with eyes of fire and feet like burnished bronze, whose voice is like many waters, and what does he do? The same thing you or I would do if we saw Him in all of His glory right now—fall on our face! Who can be compared to our God? The prophecy concerning John the Baptist is that he fulfilled Isaiah 40:3; how interesting to see it in the context of Isaiah 40.

John is describing, in part, the Day of the Lord. A day of separating the wheat from the chaff, the things of the Spirit from the things of the flesh. That which is of God remains; that which is not of God is taken away and burned. The Word says before the great Day of the Lord He would send Elijah. Why? To get people ready! In order to be ready you need to be reminded of what is coming! People may not want to hear it (most will likely not), but the Elijah Generation will be used to stir people from their slumber, because they themselves will be alert and sober, understanding, like the sons of Issachar, the signs of the times and what to do (1 Chronicles 12:32). If we know what is coming, we have a responsibility to tell people! If you knew the full expanse of devastation Hurricane Katrina or the earthquakes of Japan would bring before they came, you would warn people to flee. We are looking at something even more catastrophic, enormous, and life-altering than these terrible events.

Look at what the "Day of the Lord" is about. According to the Word:

Isaiah 2:11-22 - All arrogance will stop! The pride of man will stop! The Lord alone will be exalted in that Day! Idols will be smashed, and when He arises, the earth will shake because of the glory of His majesty.

Isaiah 13:6, 9-15 – People will howl, as it is a day of wrath and fierce anger. Sinners will be removed from the land and God will punish the world for its evil and the wicked for their sins. The Lord will shake the heavens, and the earth will be removed from its place. Isaiah states that this will be done "in the wrath of the LORD of hosts and in the day of His fierce anger." No one outside of Christ will escape this Day.

Isaiah 24 – The world will be laid waste. All will be judged; there will be no respect given to position or person. Again, no one will escape this day. The earth itself will be broken down and completely destroyed; it will reel to and fro like a drunken man. All the "joy" of the world with their drinking, partying, and music will end for those who do not repent.

Ezekiel 30 – It is a day of judgment against those who do not know God and have rebelled against Him and are in league against His people.

Joel 1:15 – A day of destruction

Joel 2:11 – A day that is terrible, who can abide it?

Joel 2:31 – The sun will be turned into darkness, the moon to blood before this Day

Joel 3:14-16 – Multitudes are seen in this valley of decision, will you be used to persuade them? The Lord will roar out of Zion!

Amos 5:18-20 – A warning to those who desire this Day to come! It is a day of darkness and not light. Again no one will escape this Day!

Zephaniah 1:7- The imminence of the Day of the Lord! Also, in the context of those worshipping the creation rather than the Creator.

Zephaniah 1:14-2:3- A day of wrath, a day of trouble, a day of distress, a day of wasteness and desolation, a day of darkness, and gloominess. The wicked's blood will be poured out like dust and their flesh will be like dung. Money will not deliver them, but all will be destroyed in the fire of His jealousy. The exhortation? Seek the Lord! Seek righteousness, seek meekness and He says,

"You will be hid in the Day of the Lord's anger."

Zephaniah 14 – The Day of the Lord's coming as relating to the Battle of Armageddon.

Matthew 24- Jesus gave clear warning and signs of the nearness of this Day.

Paul talks about it in 1 Thessalonians 5 and in 2 Thessalonians, Peter talks about in 2 Peter.

Revelation reveals specifically what this time will be like!

Some will say, "This doesn't really apply to me, I'm saved," but Peter speaks to the Church in what should be our personal response be in light of such a day:

"Seeing, then, that all these things will be dissolved, <u>what manner of person you should be in all holy conduct and godliness</u>. Looking for and hasting the coming of the Day of God, where the heavens being on fire will be dissolved and the elements will melt with fervent heat? Nevertheless, we, according to His promise, look for a new heavens and a new earth, where dwells righteousness. <u>Therefore, beloved, seeing that you look for such things, be diligent that you may be found of him in peace, without spot, and blameless.</u>"

(2 Peter 3:11—14)

<u>Be diligent</u> that you may be found in Him in peace, without spot and blameless! That's not a passive stance, but active and assertive!

Brother, are you living in light of this Truth?

It's time for the Elijah generation to speak the full counsel of God, that the blood of others would not be on our heads, and that we would be found obedient and faithful to warn others of what is coming. If we are abiding in God we will not have to fear the fire but have confidence on that day, for what comes out will be gold, silver, and precious stones (1 Corinthians 3), for the glory of God!

Jesus, help us and teach us more and more what it means to abide in You!

Father, let us speak the full counsel of Your Word, without hypocrisy or fear of man. Help this to ever be before us, may we be diligent to be found of You in peace, without spot and blameless in Jesus' Name and faithfully telling others about the Day of the Lord that is coming.

CHAPTER 27

John, a Man of Humility

And they came to John and said to him, "Rabbi,
He who was with you beyond the Jordan, to whom
you have testified— behold He is baptizing, and all
are coming to Him!" John answered and said, "A
man can receive nothing unless it has been given to
him from heaven. You yourselves bear me witness,
that I said, 'I am not the Christ,' but, 'I have been
sent before Him.' He who has the bride is the
bridegroom; but the friend of the bridegroom, who
stands and hears him, rejoices greatly because of
the bridegroom's voice. Therefore this joy of mine
is fulfilled. He must increase, but I must decrease."

John 3:26-30

Another attribute of the Elijah generation, as modeled by
John the Baptist, is that they will be men of humility.
They will understand what John means when he says, "A man can
receive nothing unless it has been given to him from heaven." This

is the understanding of humility, that a man can receive nothing that is good that does not come from God!

Paul said, "For who makes you differ from another? And what do you have that you did not receive? Now if you did indeed receive it, why do you boast as if you had not received it?" (1 Corinthians 4:7).

Paul was also clear when he states, "For you see your calling, brethren, that not many wise according to the flesh, not many mighty, not many noble, are called. But God has chosen the foolish things of the world to put to shame the wise, and God has chosen the weak things of the world to put to shame the things which are mighty; and base things of the world and the things which are despised God has chosen, and the things which are not, to bring to nothing the things that are, that no flesh should glory in His presence" (1 Corinthians 1:26-29).

Where can there be any pride in that revelation? Let it sink into our hearts, Lord!

Paul said that there is no good thing that is within us (in our flesh) (Romans 7:18, emphasis mine).

Pride wants to say, "Look at the great talents I have. Look at the spiritual gifts I have."

But the man of humility will confess out of his mouth, "All that I have that is good comes from God!"

"Every good gift and every perfect gift is from above, and comes down from the Father of lights...." (James 1:17, emphasis mine).

Jeremiah 9:23-24 declares, "Thus says the LORD: 'Let not the wise man glory in his wisdom, let not the mighty glory in his might, nor let the rich man glory in his riches; but let him who glories glory in this, that he understands and knows Me, that I am the

LORD, exercising loving-kindness, judgment, and righteousness in the earth. For in these I delight,' says the LORD."

We must be marked as men of humility; we must reject the spirit of pride. We must reject the spirit of jealousy and the spirit of competition. We must continually point people to Jesus! Do not bring attention to yourself!

Many times as soon as people see anointing, they want to lift up the man. Why? Because they are immature; they are still babes in Christ as Paul reveals in 1 Corinthians 3; they are still in the flesh. However, we should have no room to allow that to happen to us; we must continually say with John that anything in our lives that is good has come from God. We also say with John, "He must increase, but I must decrease." I must decrease, and He must increase! The anointing should not be the goal anyway. The priests of old were anointed to minister but the joy was when God's presence manifested. The anointing leads us to the glory of God, and when the glory of God comes NO man, NO one is left standing (1 Kings 8, Exodus 40)!

A sign of maturity is that we find ways in which we can humble ourselves, staying behind the cross and being careful to give God all the glory. If we stay in that place of humility, we will be in a position to receive grace from God, for He gives grace to the humble (James 4:6, 1 Peter 5:5). His grace is all we need! This was the revelation Paul received as to why he had a messenger of Satan sent to him, lest he be filled with pride (2 Corinthians 12). The safest place, the place God wants us to be, is in the place of humility. Pride is self-dependence, whereas humility is dependence on God. How can we stay in that place of humility? By being reminded of it by a daily meditation of the Word of God and by way of prayer. Every time we are praying, we are confessing our need for God. Remember, prayerlessness is nothing other than a manifestation of pride.

Just as pride is inseparably linked to prayerlessness, so humility is inseparably linked to love. When you and I are walking in true humility (and there is a false humility which focuses on oneself, speaking oneself down and beating oneself up), we find ourselves loving others and preferring them above ourselves. Paul states in Philippians 2:3-4, "Let nothing be done through selfish ambition or conceit, but in lowliness of mind let each esteem others better than himself. Let each of you look out not only his own interests, but also for the interests of others."

I want to share a testimony of how this changed my life.

I met David in Chicago and was blessed by the Holy Spirit fire that I saw in his life, and I truly experienced the reality, "As iron sharpens iron, so a man sharpens the countenance of his friend" (Proverb 27:17).

David and I would seek God's face together and have blessed times in His presence.

One day, we set up a time to seek God through the night. Because I was a youth pastor, I had the keys to the church, so we went downstairs to the youth room. We started in praise and worship; then we began to call on His Name and cry out for His glory to come. God's presence began to manifest, and eventually we found ourselves on our faces.

Sometime around three o'clock in the morning, we were both quiet before the Lord. It was then, all of a sudden, that David cried out with all of his heart, "Lord, I prefer my brother above myself! Father, whatever I've asked for myself, I ask You to give it to my brother!"

I felt the presence and love of God just hit me. I was

overwhelmed. I knew this brother. This brother had fasted for long periods of time. This brother had faithfully risen early for years to pray to God. This brother was a passionate worshipper and seeker of God's face, and this brother had experienced incredible breakthroughs with God.

Now, David was preferring me above himself? All those tears he cried, all those hours in fasting and prayer, all the desires of his heart to see the glory of God and the Kingdom come in power, he was asking for me to receive the fruit of that labor!

It was as if a wave hit me, a wave of God's Spirit. Then, this cry came out of me, "Father, I prefer my brother above myself! Whatever I've asked for, give to him!"

I testify that God honored those prayers! My life was not the same. Such is the mark of true love and true humility. It is the spirit of Jonathan who, although he had the rightful place to be king in place of his father, loved David and preferred David above himself. Such prayers will destroy the spirit of pride and the spirit of competition and jealousy! So many teachings are about ourselves..."Bless me!" — "Touch me!"

What would happen if we turned that zeal, in humility, to asking the Father to bless our brother above ourselves? Do you think we might see revival? Imagine if brothers in Christ started praying this way in all our churches. Imagine if pastors started praying this way together in city-wide or town-wide gatherings. Now imagine, whether or not you are a father, if one of your children was coming to you and telling you that he wanted you to bless his brother with whatever he himself was asking to receive, something you intended to give to him. What would that do to the heart of a father? You would be filled with such joy! You would probably bless **both** their socks off! How much more does the

Heavenly Father delight in such prayers!

Let us pray for each other to be clothed in true humility and to be looking to Jesus as our example of what it means to walk in humility (in the full consideration of Philippians 2).

We must keep the focus on Jesus. We must acknowledge that we can do nothing apart from God! We must constantly confess it!

Satan is going to come and try to get you to depend on yourself—your experience and your knowledge. The enemy is going to come and tempt you to do what David did in 1 Chronicles 21:1, i.e., to look over your shoulder at your accomplishments, to look at what you have and be lifted up in your heart—to cease depending on God and giving Him all the glory.

Be careful! The enemy knows that if he can get pride to enter our hearts, God will resist us. The Word of God clearly states that everyone proud in heart is an abomination to God, and assuredly they will not go unpunished (Proverbs 16:5).

Let us bring an example of humility, true humility.

"As the refining pot for silver and the furnace for gold, so is a man to his praise" (Proverbs 27:21).

Proverbs indicates that praise will refine you. It is a test—every time—to see what you are going to do with it. Are you going to receive it, or are you going to give glory to God?

Be careful of people who will try to build a platform for you.

Jesus said, "Without Me you can do nothing" (John 15:5). It is one thing to acknowledge that as truth; it is another thing to experientially know that to be true.

Jesus said of Himself, as our example, in John 5:19- 20, "Most assuredly, I say to you, the Son can do nothing of Himself, but what He sees the Father do; for whatever He does, the Son also does in like manner. For the Father loves the Son, and shows

Him all things that He Himself does; and He will show Him greater works than these, that you may marvel."

Father, make us men of humility who understand in our hearts, not just our minds, that apart from Jesus we can do nothing. Remove all pride from our hearts. We do not want You to resist us; we want to be able to receive the fullness of Your grace, that it might return to You in the highest praise, in Jesus' Name. Let us prefer others above ourselves in prayer and action.

CHAPTER 28

John and Elijah, Men Who Were Marked by Much Zeal

And from the days of John the Baptist until now the kingdom of heaven suffers violence, and the violent take it by force.

Matthew 11:12

Zeal – great energy or enthusiasm in pursuit of a cause or an objective. (The New Oxford American Dictionary)

The people that make an impression on this world are people of passion, people of zeal – whether for good or for evil. Look at the lives of those who lead changes, start revolutions, and bring about movements in societies. They are people of zeal who motivate others to action.

This was the mark of John and Elijah. Elijah said, "I have been very zealous for the LORD God of hosts" (1 Kings 19:10). He was zealous **for God**! – Zealous because the people of God had forsaken the covenant of God and torn down His altars.

This was also a characteristic in life of our Lord Jesus:

> *Now the Passover of the Jews was at hand, and Jesus went up to Jerusalem. And He found in the temple those who sold oxen and sheep and doves, and the moneychangers doing business. When He had made a whip of cords, He drove them all out of the temple, with the sheep and the oxen, and poured out the changers' money and overturned the tables. And He said to those who sold doves, "Take these things away! Do not make My Father's house a house of merchandise!" Then His disciples remembered that it was written, "Zeal for Your house has eaten Me up."*
>
> John 2:13-17

This generation, too, will be marked by great zeal.

God's command in Romans 12:11 is to be "fervent in spirit," which means literally to be "boiling over in spirit." This is not optional; this is a command of God.

The Spirit of God manifests as fire! We are not to put out that fire! (1 Thessalonians 5:19).

Jesus rebuked the church of Laodicea in Revelation 3 for their being lukewarm.

Brother, the way to keep from becoming lukewarm is to get near the fire. God reveals Himself as a consuming fire: "For the LORD your God is a consuming fire, a jealous God" (Deuteronomy 4:24). That is also why He says in Hebrews 1:7 that He "makes... His ministers a flame of fire."

Fire!

That is how God revealed Himself to Abraham!

That is how God came down on Mount Sinai!

That is how God manifested Himself in the Tabernacle!

That is how God came down on the Day of Pentecost!

That is how God is coming back in Revelation!

God wants us to be filled with His fire; God's heart burns, and ours should as well.

The world and the enemy are going to try to do everything to put out that fire. That is what sin does; it steals the fire from the altar of your heart. That is what laziness does; it causes the fire to subside.

When we draw near to God in worship, prayer, and coming away alone with God, we will be invigorated with the fire of God. We will be alive to the things of God!

It is also clear from Scripture that, "Two are better than one, because they have a good reward for their labor. For if they fall, one will lift up his companion. But woe to him who is alone when he falls, for he has no one to help him up. Again, if two lie down together, they will keep warm; but how can one be warm alone? Though one may be overpowered by another, two can withstand him. And a threefold cord is not quickly broken" (Ecclesiastes 4:9-12).

The command of God is that we "exhort one another daily, while it is called 'Today,' lest any of you be hardened through the deceitfulness of sin" (Hebrews 3:13, emphasis mine).

"And let us consider one another in order to stir up love and good works, not forsaking the assembling of ourselves together, as is the manner of some, but exhorting one another, and so much the more as you see the Day approaching" (Hebrews 10:25, emphasis mine).

We need each other, Brothers! There is something so powerful when brothers get together and spur one another on in prayer and exhortation. How quickly the fire can leap from one man to another.

As you know, an ember that will quickly stop burning when its separated from the rest of the coals. Stay in a place of accountability. Stay in contact with brothers of zeal. The account is that those in the Second Great Awakening would greet each other by asking, "Is the fire burning?"

When you let the fire of God burn intensely in your life, you need to know there will be added warfare. My family and I were getting ready to learn the Wolof language by moving up to a compound in northern Senegal (near the border of Mauritania). One night as I was driving with my team leader, we tried to take a short cut through the vast Savannah and got lost. It was an overcast day, so we could not see where the sun was setting in order to know which way was west. Finally, the weather broke up and we realized that we were going in the wrong direction. As we quickly tried to follow some donkey trails in the sand and brush before the sunset, we realized God was going to have to help us or we would get completely lost and run out of gas. We had no cell phone coverage; we were too far from any tower.

I remember that blackness when night came, for there was no "light pollution"—nothing. Then, far in the distance, we saw a campfire. It looked to be miles away, but you could see it clearly because there was no other light source anywhere. It stuck out like a sore thumb in the vast expanse of darkness. It was then that God spoke to me and said, "Son, this is what you look like in the spirit world." What a revelation that was to me! No wonder the spiritual warfare was so intense sometimes; it was like a lamp burning alone with all the moths and bugs being drawn to it! No doubt the brighter the light in you, the more of a threat you will be to the enemy. It will attract attention—both good and bad.

Jesus said concerning John, "He was the burning and shining lamp, and you were willing for a time to rejoice in his light" (John 5:35). **We** are the light of the world and we are to have our lamps burning (Luke 12:35).

How bright a fire do you want to be? Your brightness will depend upon your measure of surrender.

If you are going to live hot for God, you had better keep yourself in a position of dependence on God and stay close to other brothers, or you will have some unnecessary turbulent times ahead. Keep putting yourself—like David did—in a position to hear the voice of God, to receive His counsel on which way to go forward. Do not be presumptuous. I can personally testify (with many others) to several times having brushes with death in this warfare, but we must remember Jesus is the one who holds the keys of death, hell and the grave! He knows the days that are appointed to us (Psalm 139:16), and as long as we walk with Him, nothing and no one can take our lives before that appointed time.

Isaiah makes the statement that, "There is no one who calls on Your name, who stirs himself up to take hold of You" (Isaiah 64:7).

O Brothers, may this not be true of us. Let us stir ourselves up to take hold of God and His promises. The hour is urgent; is there any other option?

God says in Ezekiel 9, verse 4 (emphasis mine), "And the LORD said to him, 'Go through the midst of the city, through the midst of Jerusalem, and put a mark on the foreheads of <u>the men who sigh and cry over all the abominations that are done within</u>

it.'" All the rest were to be judged. God told Ezekiel to put a mark on those who take it to heart, those that are zealous for God, those that grieve over the condition of God's people. Such people are marked by God. They are not harboring sin in their hearts, which would cause them to be cold and indifferent.

That is so often the difference in how a war is won—one side wants it more than the other. One side sees the vision more clearly: that losing is not an option and it is all or nothing. The enemy is angry, but we should have a greater anger against him, because Jesus is worthy and the enemy has stolen the glory that belongs to God! That should put a great zeal in our hearts! The enemy steals time, souls, and glory that belong to God. That ought to stir us! There should be a fight in you, Brother! A fight that is manifested in your time of intercession and reaching out in love to those around you. Be found fighting on your knees and calling on our great God for revival to come and for the works of the enemy to be destroyed. Pray with David that the Lord would smash the teeth of the enemy! It is time to rise up, warrior! Fight the good fight of faith in prayer and intercession, calling on the Lord and using the weapons He has given you! Jesus is victorious! The Lord is your banner! Yahweh Nissi! Let us pray the prayer of Moses and David, and cry out daily, "Rise up, O LORD! Let your enemies be scattered and let those who hate You flee from before You" (Numbers 10:35, see also Psalm 68:1).

Victory is Yours, O Lord Jesus! Lead us on!

CHAPTER 29

John, a Man of Much Fasting

Then they said to Him, "Why do the disciples of John fast often and make prayers, and likewise those of the Pharisees, but Yours eat and drink?" And He said to them, "Can you make the friends of the bridegroom fast while the bridegroom is with them? But the days will come when the bridegroom will be taken away from them; then they will fast in those days.

Luke 5:33-35

God has given us great promises and revelation about the power of fasting. If you look in the Bible, when God's people fasted, it brought a quick response from heaven.

Look again at the promise of God in Isaiah 58:6: "Is this not the fast that I have chosen: to loose the bonds of wickedness, to undo the heavy burdens, to let the oppressed go free, and that you break every yoke?"

Glory! Let us agree and act upon such a promise!

Fasting is a way to humble ourselves and to have victory over our flesh, driving unbelief and doubt out of our hearts. Fasting brings us into a position to hear God's voice with more clarity. It is a gift from God that can be used to help us draw closer to Him.

It is also a sign of humiliation. Fasting demonstrates that we are greatly in need of God, so that our inner man can be strengthened and fortified to resist sin and temptation.

Fasting makes us more sensitive to things of God and the things contrary to God. It can be like a fire, causing the junk, selfish ambitions, and things of the flesh to rise up so that God can scrape them from our lives.

Fasting is used to maintain passion. God honors fasting, if it is done in the way Jesus describes in Matthew 6, i.e., unto God and not unto man.

If we want to be a part all God wants us to be as part of preparing the way for His return, then we too must be a people of fasting. There is power in fasting, and the enemy knows it. How he fights against the people of God who understand this! He wants to keep the stomachs of the people of God constantly filled and overflowing in order to keep them satisfied and keep their vision limited.

How is it that Muslims, who have not the Spirit of God, fast more than the children of God most of the time? Try to explain that. Something is wrong, terribly wrong. Muslims fast a month out of every year. Is it any wonder that they are so zealous and that their zeal often seems so much more intense than that of many believers in Jesus in the Western church? There is a spiritual authority that comes with fasting. I was amazed how even many missionaries that I worked with in Muslim countries did not discern this. We, by the power of the Spirit, should be more zealous in fasting than they and counter their fleshly, demonic fasts with the fasting in the power of the Spirit. It is going to bring a breakthrough!

Many American believers are concerned how quickly Islam is spreading in America and how far it has already advanced in Europe. Many will complain about it, many have fear about it, but few are doing something about it. One of the ways we are going to see victory is through fasting. We will receive power from God to move into the supernatural, and through fasting we will put ourselves in a position, where God can use us see salvation come to the Muslims. We should be praying that He would be gracious to Muslims and even give them dreams and visions. We should pray that we ourselves would be bold to speak the Word of God. He alone is the Way, the Truth, and the Life. No one comes to the Father but by Him (John 14:6).

I will state again what I stated in chapter 2 (concerning Scripture memorization); a lot of the church is just plain lazy and indulent! We can be some of the most undisciplined people. The word "discipline" has almost become a dirty word in some circles. Mention the word and you are sometimes perceived as "old school" and still under law and not under grace—amazing. What it reveals, again, is a lack of Biblical knowledge and too much of a dependency on being fed by others rather than being students of the Word of God. Paul told Timothy, a leader, a pastor who was to be an example to all, "Discipline yourself for the purpose of godliness" (1 Timothy 4:7 NASB, emphasis mine). Paul, with transparency, revealed of himself in 1 Corinthians 9, "Do you not know that those who run in a race all run, but one receives the prize? Run in such a way that you may obtain it. And everyone who competes for the prize is temperate in all things. Now they do it to obtain a perishable crown, but we for an imperishable crown. Therefore I run thus: not with uncertainty. Thus I fight: not as one who beats the air. But I underline{discipline} my body and bring it into subjection, lest, when I have preached to others, I myself should become disqualified" (9:24-27, emphasis mine).

We are to be like Jesus. Do people not think Jesus was a man of discipline? How easy it is to fall into preaching that tends to help us find "the easy way out." We create theology to make things easier on ourselves. I have nothing against times of "soaking," but we are not going to win the world for Christ while spending most of our time on our backs.

There is also a wrestling in prayer, according to the Bible, and anyone who tells you otherwise has not come to a place of full revelation on prayer. It was said of Jesus Himself that He offered loud cries and tears and He was heard because of His reverent submission (Hebrews 5:7). Paul talks about "groanings" (Romans 8:26) and travailing in prayer (Galatians 4:19). Fasting was constantly a part of Paul's life; look again at 2 Corinthians 11, "in fastings often." How much our culture can affect us. Go overseas and into a Muslim country and live there to start a work for God and see how long you can go before you are going to have to discipline yourself, whether in language study, prayer, fasting, or evangelism. You are not always going to "feel like it." You do it because it is obedience, because it is the right thing to do. Should not the same truth be applied regardless of where we live? Would not the principle of discipline bear even more fruit in our country where there is less overt spiritual warfare?

Many men of God throughout history can testify how much fasting changed them and how it quickly brought them to a place where God could pour out His grace and power to glorify Himself and advance His Kingdom. I highly recommend Bill Bright's

Fasting For the Coming Revival as a simple, practical guide to fasting and a book of encouragement. It gives practical counsel and is filled with testimonies and encouragement. Allow God to take you on a journey of faith through fasting, going from fasting a single meal, to fasting a day, to fasting seven days, to perhaps even fasting three weeks or 40 days. The Bible says, "You have not because you ask not." Ask God for grace and empowerment to fast and grow in fasting, and He will answer your prayer.

I have heard so many use the excuse that they do not "feel led" to fast. The Word of God states in James 4:8 that we are to draw near to God and He will draw near to us. It does **not** say, God draws near to us and we draw near to God. The initiation is with us! We have as much of God as we want. So many are "waiting" for something to fall out of the sky, something to just hit them, that makes them want to fast. God gives grace, but we must respond to the Word. **You** must stir up the gift, **you** must seek the face of God, and **you** must initiate fasting; it is not just going to "happen." Jesus is inviting us to fast, but He also is expecting us to fast. The Word does not say in Matthew 6, "If you fast," but rather, "When you fast." As someone has said, "It is hard to steer a parked car." In the same way, why would we expect God to give us grace to fast if there is no asking or movement to do so on our part.

I can state with total conviction, "Fasting will change you," because it comes out of experience, not theory or head knowledge. I am a different man because of the discipline of fasting. I assure you, you will never regret a day you fasted. You will not look back at the end of your life and say, "I wish I hadn't fasted so much!" If it is done in the Spirit, it will prove to have eternal fruit. If it is done in the Spirit, you will actually find yourself at times in great joy while you fast. It is time to discipline ourselves, Brothers, to prepare ourselves and our families for the coming of the Lord.

May more and more churches grab hold of the Biblical understanding of the "solemn assembly" and call for corporate fasts. Do you not think God will answer such an offering of incense before His throne? Will that incense not fill those bowls and be poured out in lightning, thunder, and earthquakes of His power and glory as He glorifies His Son and revives His people for His namesake? O Father, give us more grace, we ask, and let us throw off every excuse, in Jesus' Name! No more excuses! Let us follow Your example and expectation, Jesus! You said that when the Bridegroom is taken, then, in those days, your followers would fast. Start in us, as we fast in secret to be seen by You, but also may Your Church be mobilized to fast corporately and see the heavens open! In Jesus' Name!

My challenge for the brothers is to join with many other brothers who are fasting every Friday at a minimum, to set apart every Friday to fast for our lives, our families, our churches, and for world evangelism. It also happens to be Islam's holy day. Is there a greater challenge facing the church in this hour? If they come in the authority of fasting 30 days of the year, we as God's children will at least be found fasting 52 days out of the year. We will see doors open to share with Muslims.

Father, we ask again, give us more grace to fast more, that we might be fitted vessels, channels of Your grace and power, and filled with mountain-moving faith. May Your Church arise and fast corporately. Give pastors and church leaders boldness and vision to proclaim fasts, to see You glorified, to see unity in the church, to see protection and blessing over marriages and children, and to see Your kingdom come and Your will be done on earth as it is in heaven. In Jesus' Name, we pray.

CHAPTER 30

John: Faithful to Death

For Herod had laid hold of John and bound him, and put him in prison for the sake of Herodias, his brother Philip's wife. Because John had said to him, "It is not lawful for you to have her." And although he wanted to put him to death, he feared the multitude, because they counted him as a prophet.

Matthew 14:3-5

So he sent and had John beheaded in prison.

Matthew 14:10

"Be faithful until death." These were the words of Jesus in Revelation 2 to the church of Smyrna. The church was suffering under heavy persecution; does it not strike you that Jesus does not spend any words comforting them or expressing words of deep sorrow for their plight? He simply says that He knows their tribulation and then says, "Do not fear any of those things which you are about to suffer. Indeed, the devil is about to throw some of you into prison, that you may be tested, and you will have tribulation ten days. Be faithful until death, and I will give you the crown of life" (Revelation 2:10).

We are to be ready to die for the testimony of our Lord. This is the expectation of Jesus, for if we try to save our lives, we will lose them. Jesus said this is the victory we have over the devil. "'And they overcame him by the blood of the Lamb and by the word of their testimony, and they did not love their lives to the death,'" (Revelation 12:11).

Put yourself in the position of one of Jesus' first disciples. You are excited to go out; Jesus is sending you! He has given you power to heal the sick and cast out demons and even raise the dead! The excitement is growing as Jesus tells you that you will be going house to house and you will have to depend on Him even for your food. Then He says you are to shake the dust off your feet of those towns that do not receive you. You think, "Okay, we are going to face some rejection… I can handle that."

Then Jesus tells you, "But beware of men, for they will deliver you up to councils and scourge you in their synagogues...."

What?! Did He say scourge? Your mind starts envisioning this—but wait, Jesus is still speaking. "And you will be hated by all for My name's sake. But he who endures to the end will be saved. When they persecute you in this city, flee to another."

Are you ready to go, Brother? That is what Jesus expected the first time He sent out His disciples.

Toward the end of their time with Jesus, He spoke even more plainly. "Then they will deliver you up to tribulation and kill you, and you will be hated by all nations for My name's sake. And then many will be offended, will betray one another, and will hate one another" (Matthew 24:9-10).

Look at the perspective of the men of God of old, who "were tortured, not accepting deliverance, that they might obtain a better resurrection" (Hebrews 11:35). Let that one sink into your spirit.

Do you see how far we have come? What is wrong? Part of what has happened is that the church has not evoked persecution because the church has not been a threat to the devil or his kingdom.

Continual prayer in churches? Most of our churches have coffee houses rather than houses built just for prayer. Many will say, "Our coffee houses are for outreach." Jesus commands us to go, and if that is the environment you want to see new believers birthed in, then prepare for an uphill battle in getting them fired up about boldly preaching the Gospel.

Regular fasting? Most of our churches pride themselves on their potluck dinners or chili cook-offs.

Weekly evangelism? Most of our church bulletins are filled with activities, fun outings, or seminars rather than opportunities to reach the lost.

Let us get real with each other. This is a far cry from Matthew 10 and Jesus' first commissioning His disciples to go and preach the Kingdom of God. I have discovered, with many other brothers, that the front line is in evangelism. That is where the warfare is, and that is where you will see the miracles of Jesus (notice again the context of Mark 16:15-20). Look at the book of Acts; when Paul preached, that is when the sparks started to fly. If he had quietly gone about his business or was content with only friendship evangelism, no doubt things would not have been stirred up like they were.

Does it bother you, Brother, that we are not seeing what the church of Acts saw? Or do I sound "out of touch?" We must remember that the standard on that final Day is the Word of God, which is above any cultural influence.

It starts with surrender and submission. It starts with a heart position that tells Jesus, "I'll follow you wherever You lead. Jesus, I'm willing to go anywhere You want me to go." We must grow up like Peter did as Jesus revealed this aspect of spiritual maturity, "Most assuredly, I say to you, when you were younger, you girded yourself and walked where you wished; but when you are old, you will stretch out your hands, and another will gird you and carry you where you do not wish" (John 21:18). There is a spiritual principal in this verse!

In the meantime, or if God is not calling us to this right now, we are to pray for those who are facing persecution and martyrdom now.

Hebrews 13:3 states, "Remember the prisoners as if chained with them—those who are mistreated—since you yourselves are in the body also."

I would strongly suggest that every Christian home should have a copy of Foxe's Book of Martyrs along with John Bunyan's Pilgrim's Progress. We must return to our roots! We must prepare ourselves, for the time is upon us now! As the organization Voice of the Martyrs points out, approximately every three minutes someone is martyred for his or her faith! Think on that for a moment. Take that in; let it enter your heart. We need to educate our children. When we do, most persecution we (or they) might face will be brought into the appropriate perspective.

When I was a missionary in Senegal, I went to a gathering called the "Stephen's Conference." A man who was a missionary in Somalia for some time led it. Within 24 hours, he saw 200 of the Somalian believers killed for their faith. He realized that fanatical

Muslims were able to find these believers, in part, by following his activities. This servant of God was broken by his experience and he was trying to use it to help other missionaries to act with greater wisdom. He had seen much persecution, and as he traveled over the world speaking at these conferences, he saw more and more. I will never forget one of his testimonies.

He said that when he went to the Chinese underground church, he shared with them about persecution that believers were experiencing in other parts of the world, specifically in Saudi Arabia and Somalia. As he kept sharing, he was struck that there was absolutely no visible reaction from the Chinese believers; their faces were as still as stone. He started to wonder if he was even being interpreted correctly. They closed the meeting and he headed out to go to bed.

While it was still dark, he was awakened by banging and shouting. He thought for sure that the police had found the meeting, and that they were coming to make arrests! With his heart racing, he quickly made his way to where the sound was coming from, but when he opened the door, he found the Chinese brothers and sisters on their faces, crying, pounding the floor, yelling to heaven. He still did not understand, but as he listened he began to hear the words "Saudi Arabia" and "Somalia." When he asked his interpreter what was happening, he was told that the Chinese believers had met together after the missionary had left. They had agreed together to rise an hour early to pray for their brothers and sisters in Saudi Arabia and Somalia! They had already been getting up at 5:00 am; and they themselves were also facing persecution! Brothers, this is love. Love moves us to do something about that which we receive. The missionary said it was no surprise that some weeks after this event, they started to hear of changes taking place among the persecuted churches in these countries. God hears the cries of His children. How He must have been moved with such compassion at the cries of these Chinese brothers and sisters of ours!

Brothers, let us do the same; let us not be spectators, but participants. May we say with Paul that Christ shall be glorified in us by life or by death.

Are you ready to follow Jesus, no matter the distance? We must give our all to Jesus. We only have one life, one chance; let us give it all for God. Let us hold nothing back, for our Lord held nothing back from us.

Worthy is the Lamb who was slain to receive the reward of His suffering! HalleluYah!!!

It is time for the Elijah Generation to arise.

Father, may we be found faithful until death. May we not love our lives even to death. May we be found faithful in praying for our brothers and sisters in prison and under severe persecution in the same way we would want them to pray for us—as if we ourselves were in chains. Spirit of God, we ask You to bring this to our continual remembrance, in Jesus' Name.

Give me one hundred preachers who fear nothing but sin, and desire nothing but God, and I care not a straw whether they be clergymen or laymen; such alone will shake the gates of hell and set up the kingdom of heaven on Earth.

John Wesley, Founder of the Methodist Church

Week #5
Discussion questions and points of application

1. Have you or someone you know been influenced or injured by a religious spirit/ environment? Pray for them, and prayerfully write a letter or make a call or set up a time to simply speak blessings and life over them and share with them their identity in Christ. Be an agent of Christ's healing.

2. In prayer ask God to teach each one how to abide in Christ. Why do you think so many of our churches don't talk about the Day of the Lord? How can there be a healthy balance to be reminded of it and yet live in joy? What example do you see of that in Scripture?

3. What ways can we fulfill the God's command to "Humble yourself"? Give specific situations as examples.

4. Set a time at the end of our meeting to pray for each other and prefer each other. Whatever you would want for God to do in your life, pray that over your brother in Jesus Name.

5. What are some specific characteristics of someone who is zealous for what they believe in? How would see that applied to the Christian life?

6. If you have seen the power of fasting testify. Prayerfully consider setting a day to fast together (even if you can't

be together) for your families, the church, or the lost around you.

7. In what way are you actively supporting the persecuted church? Visit the websites of Voices of the Martyrs or Persecution Project and others to find out how you can get involved. We are the Body of Christ.

A Final Comment About the Life of Elijah

One may (rightly) point out that Elijah was not perfect. He fell into great depression, during which he asked God to take his life (1 Kings 19:4). Scripture is clear to reveal all aspects of men of God, their victories and defeats. The Bible says of Elijah that he was a man subject to similar passions as we are (James 5:17). We will all have our breaking points, where we will come to a revelation of our weakness and frailty (and possibly even come to a place of despair). Yet even when we are disbelieving, God remains faithful because He cannot deny Himself (2 Timothy 2:13).

I believe we must remember three things in response to this time of weakness in Elijah's life. First, God is so gracious; He came to minister to Elijah and drew near to him in that dark hour. God remembers that our frame is but dust. He is near to the broken-hearted and saves the crushed in spirit (Psalm 34:18). Second, the context of this confession is crucial, for Elijah said, "I have been very zealous for the LORD God of hosts; for the children of Israel have forsaken Your covenant, torn down Your altars, and killed Your prophets with the sword. I alone am left; and they seek to take my life" (1 Kings 19:10, 14). The enemy is a master of trying to isolate us, or at least making us feel like we are isolated. Satan is called a roaring lion seeking one whom he can devour (1 Peter 5:8). As many have observed, lions hunt by chasing a herd of prey until one of the animals falls away from the group and becomes isolated.

How did God respond? God told him that he was not alone! He told him of his plan to use Jehu and Elisha to execute justice. He also told him that 7,000 had, in fact, not bowed down to Baal (and thus to Jezebel's ways). That is why I believe so strongly in what I wrote in chapter 28: that we need each other. This is so crucial to our victory and to our spiritual alertness. We need to create a network of those of like mind and spirit, those whom Scripture speaks of in Malachi 3:16 (emphasis mine), "Then those who feared the LORD spoke often one to another; and the Lord hearkened, and heard it, and a book of remembrance was written before him for them that feared the Lord, and that thought upon His Name."

I can testify, as many others can, that I have seen the most rapid and radical changes take place in my life while I was assembled with other men of God who were seeking His holy face. These victories must also be maintained through accountability relationships with other godly men.

Lastly, we must remember the words of Paul, where he urges us to not only confess our weakness, but to even boast of it. "And He said to me, 'My grace is sufficient for you, for My strength is made perfect in weakness.' Therefore, most gladly I will rather boast in my infirmities, that the power of Christ may rest upon me. Therefore I take pleasure in infirmities, in reproaches, in needs, in persecutions, in distresses, for Christ's sake. For when I am weak, then am I strong" (2 Corinthians 12:9-10). The devil knows our weaknesses and will seek to exploit them, but we can confess and actually boast with Paul that when we are weak, then we are strong. Jesus receives all the more glory, for we know the victory we experience has come because of our trusting in His strength, not ours, and His grace, which is more than sufficient. We have a fuller revelation than Elijah because of our knowledge of the promises found in the New Covenant, sealed by the blood of the Son of God. When all is said and done, the Father, the Son, and the Holy Spirit are with us. We are never alone, amen?

Part of My Testimony

I grew up with good parents, who loved me unconditionally and sought to instill character in my life. As amazing as my parents were (and I could not ask for better ones!), they came to Christ later in life and thus began the journey of knowing who they were in Christ later. I do not believe my father came to Christ until I was six or seven. As new believers, they did not know how to empower me with spiritual authority and to equip me to face and resist wickedness. At seven years of age, something deeply impacted my life and opened the door for the enemy. I was out playing with some boys in the neighborhood when one of the boys, who was two years older than me, invited everyone back to his house to check out a movie. I went along with the small group, absolutely clueless as to what I was about to be exposed to. It was a pornographic video. My little mind could not get around exactly what I was watching. But something very spiritual was taking place, and it was evil. That was the beginning, and as the Scripture says, "Bad company corrupts good character." No matter what character my parents were trying to instill in me, it was not able to empower me against all that I would be exposed to by my friends who came from homes who did not know Jesus. I was with them for hours, in school and outside of school. I was exposed to more pornography and all kinds of violent, immoral movies, full of vulgarity (that many, unfortunately, would not even wince at today). I began to listen to gangster rap at age eleven and just about every kind of vile, ungodly thing was entering my ears and eyes. I remember, even at that young age, having an almost out-of-body experience and looking at myself and saying, "You are messed up." My mouth poured out all the things that were in my heart and mind. I was lost. "As he thinks in his heart, so he is" (Proverb 23:7).

When I was ten my mother had been led to a church that preached the Word of God with anointing. It took almost two years before something penetrated my darkened mind. It was July 1987, as a preacher preached against sin and explained the great price that Jesus paid for me, that my ears were opened. I still remember the challenge, "Are you too proud to confess that you're a sinner and that you need to have a personal relationship with God?" It shot through me. I remember sitting there, 12 years of age, next to a friend and beginning to tremble. I actually remember asking myself, "Why am I shaking like this?" It was then that I heard the voice of God, telling me to put my pride aside and come forward and give my life to Jesus. So, in front of about three hundred people, I turned to my friend and said, "I'm going forward." I got up and walked down that aisle. When I began to pray with the preacher, I just cried and cried, confessing my sin, and experienced the new birth and the washing of the Blood of Jesus. I felt like I could have jumped through the ceiling (which was pretty high). I was born again! I could sense the presence of the Holy Spirit! I saw everything in a new light!

I immediately went back and told my friends that they needed to repent and turn their lives to Jesus. I was not prepared for the response. Instead of them seeing this great life and wanting Jesus, they rejected the message. I even found that their parents were looking at me differently (no doubt because of the report their sons were giving them about me, telling them, I'm sure, how "bad" they were). And so, when persecution began to come, I shut up. I was not taught to expect that, to embrace that, to know that it was the path of Jesus. For several years I was quiet, and slowly, but surely, compromise set in. I realized I was still having these thoughts of lust. I do not recall anyone talking to me about having victory in my thought life. I watched all the movies everyone else was watching, full of sexual innuendoes, violence, immorality, taking God's name in vain, etc. I continued to listen to secular music and was influenced by listening to it for hours—all the popular 50's to '90s bands.

At age seventeen, something began to move in my heart again, awakening me to see my compromised condition. I began to read the Word more and found my faith increasing. It was then that Pastor Stewart Deal's words began to penetrate my heart, "Wade, you have to get in the Word, and the Word has to get in you." I still would not fully respond to that challenge for a couple more years. For though some of my convictions grew stronger and I was leading prayer before the football games, I was anything but "on fire for Jesus." I was accommodating and content to be a nice guy and good friend, but not a speaker of truth or a proclaimer of the Gospel. It was over these years that my mind continued to condemn me—lustful thoughts, thoughts that were so contrary to what I knew to be of God. How could I get free? I knew this was no way to live, constantly under a feeling of condemnation and self-defeat.

I would fast and make promises to God only to find myself

back in the gutter of lustful and ungodly thoughts again. I then went off to college. By the end of my freshman year, while playing rugby, I realized that I could go either way, towards God or towards the world. Praise God, a black inner-city pastor came to speak to our Intervarsity group. He had the same spirit as Pastor Deal; he was a man of the Word and fire. I was drawn to him and soon came to find myself as one of just two or three other whites in that precious, God-fearing congregation. It was there that I experienced the glory of God, and my life was changed.

I heard God say to me, "Son, if you will memorize My Word, I will take those thoughts out of your mind and replace them with My voice." Oh, to hear the voice of God!

I made the excuses many make at first: that I was not a good memorizer, not an exceptional student, etc. But, if God calls us to something (and He has called us all to do this), then He will help us to fulfill what He commands. I will never forget the first verse I memorized. For some reason I chose Proverbs 4:18. When I had memorized that, I went after another one, then another, then another. I would put the verses on index cards, the front having the reference, the back with the verse written out. I would put them in my pocket and pull them out through the day. After having memorized about 20 verses or so, I began to see something happening: a spiritual transformation. I realized my mind was clearer and my thoughts were not like they had been before. I realized that I was walking in victory!

Finally, one night—I will never forget it; it was my sophomore year in college—the enemy came to me. I had been sleeping, and I awoke from a sexual dream in which I was being very strongly tempted. When I awoke, I felt the presence of the enemy. He was in the room. I spoke out loud, "You couldn't tempt me to sin while

I was awake, and so you tried to come and tempt me to sin while I was sleeping. YOU FAILED!"

I felt the Spirit of God rise up in me, and I rebuked him in the Name of Jesus. Something happened in me; the victory was sealed. I was delivered from the spirit of lust, that spirit of Jezebel that had so controlled my life and made me like an Ahab. I was free! I, once again, felt like I could jump through the roof! As I kept devouring and memorizing the Word, I found my authority growing. I felt like I could push walls down; the Word was truly like fire in my bones.

It was at this same time that I met about seven other brothers who were hungry for God. We would meet together in one of the brothers' apartments to read the Word together, worship, and seek God's face. We did not know what to expect; we just knew we were hungry and that the Sunday church service by itself was not satisfying us. It was in one of those meetings that God dealt strongly with me, for though I had experienced this breakthrough, there were still "doors" that were open in my life, by which the world and enemy could enter, that I was not fully aware of.

One day, one of the brothers and I were crying out to God. I still remember our prayer, "God we're not leaving here until You change us!" It was bold, but it was with hearts that were full of love for Him and wanting to be like Him. The glory of God fell. I remember that I even had difficulty breathing, as all I could utter (almost in a whisper) was, "Holy!" I remember that after His presence started to lift, I turned to a brother. As we talked, we discovered that God had been speaking to us the very same thing in that moment! He was showing me how many things that I called "entertainment" and thought were "not that bad" were actually an abomination to Him. This was a door for the enemy to come back. He started to show me that some movies, music, and TV shows that I had watched or listened to (which were accepted by wide audiences and would seem harmless to many) were areas of compromise. He showed me that His Name being used in vain even one time was unacceptable to Him and how often in movies scantily dressed women appeared that were designed to be seductive and open the door for unclean thoughts. He showed me how influential the music I was listening to was and how the lyrics revealed a world view that was really anti-Christ and anti-Biblical. He wanted my meditation to completely align with His Word, character, and desires (and so obey Philippians 4:8). I repented and went back through all my possessions and began to break and trash a lot of store-bought music and movies and books. After I finished, it was like I could sense the smile of heaven and a new level of freedom, one that was real (and time has proven it was real).

I was so free, in fact, that I seriously thought I was called to be celibate. I felt no desire to have a wife at that time, and I was convinced that I would be single for the rest of my life. Although I thought I would return to play football in college, God had other plans. To make a long story short, by a miraculous sign, God led me to go with YWAM (Youth With A Mission) out in Salem, Oregon. I remember announcing to the class that I felt called to be single, not knowing that a young lady named Katie who was there listening would one day become my wife! But that is another story....

One of the outreaches we were a part of in YWAM was the Portland Rescue Mission. I was assigned to the basement area to work with a mildly mentally handicapped man to sort out vegetables and other food items for the homeless who would come. I remember I almost felt sorry for this man, who was very slow and strained in his speech. At one point, I looked on the wall and I saw a list of Scriptures posted there. I asked this man, Reggie, "What are these verses for?" He said that they were the memory verses for the mission. I asked, "You know these?" He said, "Yes." I then asked, "What about this one?" as I pointed randomly to a verse on the list. Then this man, who had difficultly articulating the simplest of sentences, spoke the entire verse in the King James Version, word for word, without interruption. I asked, "What about this one?" Again—perfect, no hesitation, no stumbling—it was like it was automatic. Then I said, "And this one?" Again, perfect. I asked, "Do you know all of these?" to which he simply replied, "Yes."

All of a sudden, I heard the voice of God say to me, "Son, I have given you a good mind; you are without excuse."

Needless to say, I asked for a copy of that sheet of paper and set myself to memorize those verses as well! (The same list of Scripture is found in Appendix A). I have continued to memorize, and each time I do, more faith arises, more victory, more testimonies. The Word of God brings victory! HalleluYah!

Brother, that was over eighteen years ago, and I have not looked back. I have walked in victory from that spirit of lust, from that Jezebel. I am not saying that I have not been tempted (obviously), but I have victory: victory over my thought life and victory over temptation. I could tell you some crazy testimonies how the enemy has tried to tempt me in this area, but God's Word is true in 1 Corinthians 10:13. O, how wonderful it is to walk in the Spirit of God and not be like an Ahab! The spirit of Elijah will rise up, and you will use what the enemy has sought to use to destroy you to instead become a testimony of liberation, so that other men may be set free from those same cords of sin and bondage.

I testify to you, as many others can testify, that just as God honored Phinehas for taking up the spear and pinning sin to the ground (see Chapter 1), God will give you a covenant of peace. I have walked in such peace! There is nothing like the peace of God! It surpasses all understanding! And, like Phinehas, I testify to you that God will bless your children! What a joy it is to be able to see my children walk in holiness and be so sensitive to the Spirit of God! My daughter, Abigail, has such a sensitive heart to God, so sensitive to what is pure and what is not pure. My sons, Caleb and Josiah, also walk in great conviction as to what is holy!

I remember my son, Caleb, at as early as four years of age, demonstrating such conviction. While we were living in Charlotte, we went to a family restaurant. A television was mounted in the upper corner of the room near the booth we were sitting in. Caleb turned to me and wanted to confirm, for my back was to the television, that what was playing on it was not appropriate to see. As I turned to look, I saw that it was the typical commercial, using sex appeal to sell a product. I told him it was, indeed, inappropriate. He immediately turned his head away from it and would not look back. The waitress came, asking for our order. After we had given it, my four year old son asked the waitress, "Are you a Christian?" With a sweet Southern accent, she replied, "Well yes, honey, I am!" To this, Caleb quickly responded, "Then why is that on?" and he pointed to the television.

I had to explain to Caleb that our waitress was not the owner of the restaurant, and I apologized to the waitress. She was not in the least offended, but rather was blessed.

I remember another incident when Caleb was seven years old or so. We had just been to Wal-Mart to buy a few things and I was looking for him in our house. I found him in our living room, listening to worship music that he had turned on, with his eyes closed and his hands out to God. I asked him why he was led to do this at that moment. He said he was so troubled because his eyes had seen an inappropriate magazine cover in the checkout line. He just cried, wanting to make sure his heart and mind were clean before God! (It brings tears to my eyes as I see God's faithfulness, for it was at that same age that the enemy came into my own life, and now I was seeing my son have victory over the enemy!)

I told him I was blessed for his running to God in worship, but he must also exercise authority, and command the enemy to leave.

As he took authority over the enemy and rebuked him, he looked at me with a peace and said, in regards to the image he had seen, "It's gone."

Over time, he now has modeled that to our youngest son, Josiah, and together they are quick to hold each other accountable to call sin, sin! Are they somber-faced children, constantly judging things? On the contrary! They are full of laughter and joy! They are full of life! And they are full of love! They love God and they love others with such depth for their age that, at times, it just humbles me. We often quote that Jesus was anointed with joy more then His brethren, but many forget the context of what it says in the beginning of that same verse that explains why He was anointed with such gladness (see Psalm 45:7).

Brother, God's Word is true; He will not only give that covenant of peace to you, but to your descendents!

Brother, cut off all feeding tubes, all the things that feed the flesh. God's standard is not man's standard. You need to invite the Holy Spirit into every part of your heart and home. It is time to clean house. It is time to go all out. It is time to renew our minds by the Word of God so that we will not be conformed to the pattern of this world. I was told, "You can't really get victory from this!" That is a lie from the pit of hell. God has called us to walk in freedom and victory, and His expectation is clear in Scripture: "As His divine power has given to us all things that pertain to life and godliness, through the knowledge of Him who called us by glory and virtue, by which have been given to us exceedingly great and precious promises, that through these you may be partakers of the divine nature, having escaped the corruption that is in the world through lust" (2 Peter 1:3-4).

I pray His richest blessing on you in Jesus' Name. May His love abound more and more for Him and for one another. I send my love to you in Jesus' Name and pray that whatever God has done in my life would be given double fold in your own life by Him. Father, I prefer my brother above myself. Do something even greater than what You have done in my life, Father, for Your glory! In Jesus' Name!

The principal fight of the Christian is with the world, the flesh, and the devil. These are his never-dying foes. These are the three chief enemies against whom he must wage war. Unless he gets the victory over these three, all other victories are in vain. Do not be dismayed. Greater is He that is for you than all they that be against you. Everlasting liberty or everlasting captivity are the alternatives before you. Choose liberty, and fight to the last. — BISHOP J. C. RYLE

Sin hath the devil for its father, shame for its companion, and death for its wages. —THOMAS WATSON

To what may a sinner be compared? To one who beholds open handcuffs and places his hands into them. —A SAYING FROM THE JERUSALEM TALMUD

Sin is the dare of God's justice, the rape of His mercy, the jeer of His patience, the slight of His power, and the contempt of His love. —JOHN BUNYAN

> *May the Spirit of Elijah, beloved reader, be upon us. If we seek for it we will have it. Oh, may the God of Elijah answer by fire, and consume the spirit of worldliness in the churches, burn up the dross, and make us whole-hearted Christians. May that Spirit come upon us; let that be our prayer in our family altars and in our closets. Let us cry mightily to God that we may have a double portion of the Holy Spirit, and that we may not rest satisfied with this worldly state of living, but let us, like Sampson, shake ourselves and come out from the world, that we may have the power of God."*
>
> D.L. Moody (Secret Power, Fleming Revell Company, New York, 1881, p.52)

A Proposal

If we reach the cities, we reach the nation. But if we fail in the cities, they become a cesspool that will infect the entire country.

Moody

"How are we going to see what you all are seeing in Africa happen here in America?" This is a question I have been asked in reference to the many souls surrendering to Jesus and the power of God manifest in miracles. The obstacles are clear: sports, entertainment, the Internet, mp3 players, materialism, busyness, and the list goes on. Yes, we do live in a unique age because of the extensiveness of distracting technology, but the Lord is not limited, and He is doing extraordinary things in spite of these obstacles. History has a tendency to repeat itself, and there is truth in Solomon's observation, "There is nothing new under the sun." There have always been distractions (they just take on different forms), and one can look at history and see a lot of similarities, but we can also see how God worked in spite of them. One of the greatest "revivals" in recent church history that affected entire nations came through a man named William Booth, who founded the Salvation Army. In spite of the distractions and obstacles of wealth, politics, work, indifference, coldness in the Church, etc., God moved in power and shook a nation through the Salvation Army. Few movements had such a rapid, immense, and lasting impact in all of church history as the Salvation Army had. I believe, with many others, that God wants to restore again the vision He gave Booth.

William Booth's strategy was to put God's power and grace on display by going to the worst part of the city, the darkest section, so that His light could shine for many to see. He would say, "Go for sinners, and go for the worst." When those "hopelessly" addicted and bound would convert, he would have them share their testimonies and see many others come to Jesus who battled the same addiction or attitude or situation. If people saw the grace of God reach such horrible situations, imagine how many more would believe in His ability to save them. "The testimony of Jesus is the spirit of prophecy" (Revelation 19:10).

The church has largely retreated from the inner city. Instead of reaching out to the changing demographics, they sold their prime real estate (prime especially to God because of their proximity to the lost!) and built their palaces in the suburbs. The churches went beyond a lack of vision; it was a sin that they retreated. The government and its programs have also failed to bring any real lasting change to the inner city.

It is time, time for God's sons to go into the inner city, filled with the love of God, clothed in the power of the Holy Spirit, armed with truth of God's Word, to bring the Kingdom of God. This is what Booth did with his fellow "soldiers of the Cross," and through the transformation of those rough areas of the East part of London, he gained the attention of the masses and those in leadership. Thus he was able to open the door for the Salvation Army to even be able to see laws passed that affected all of England (and spilled over into America).

Why do so many men not go forward in the things of God? I believe, in part, there is often a lack of challenge and vision. I believe God has put within men a desire for adventure, to take risks, and to do something cutting edge. Men want to be a part of something bigger than themselves, something that will bring true change. I believe there is also a desire to experience true brotherhood.

Some men will bow to fear and not take that extra step of risk, but to those who do not, when they take that extreme challenge for the glory of God, it not only brings change to others, it changes them. That adrenaline experience becomes the highlight of their year and it is what they look forward to do again. Men begin to look past the 9 to 5 and gain a higher vision, an eternal vision. I of course am not talking about climbing a mountain or finding our identity in "Braveheart," but pulling people from the fire that they might be saved as we preach the Gospel to them (Jude 23). The men that go out to evangelize will then bring that passion and vision back to their families, and it will in turn effect the next generation, as their children see the fire in the hearts of their fathers. Men will stop living vicariously through sports and being intoxicated with entertainment, and live for what will endure the fire of God on that great Day. They will have a testimony (or should I say, testimonies).

Are you ready to lose your life for the Gospel? Not just read about the intensity of the book of Acts, but live it? Are you ready to stop living just a plain, comfortable (really quite uneventful) life and step out on the "water?" Do you not want a testimony? Do you not want to just see "what would happen if...," and take that risk? Are you ready to give an account of your life to God? Are you ready to die and face God? If not, then what will make you ready? Living out the American dream? Will that satisfy you? Have you no concern for others to be saved? As Charles Spurgeon said, if you have no concern for others to be saved, you can be sure you yourself are not saved. There is no way we can continue to sit on our couches and watch hours of television, watching the world go to hell around us, and expect to have the smile of God on our life and think we are ready for the Day of Accounting. We are deceiving ourselves. This is what Jesus tried to warn us of many times (such as in Luke 12:15-21 and 12:35-48).

So I have a proposal for you brother. Are you ready to get radical and get a group to take the Gospel to the darkest part of your city? I dare you. What do you have to lose? Your life? If you stay in fear, then you are still trying to save your life and Jesus said that you will end up losing it (Luke 17:33). If you belong to Jesus, you have already died, so there really is not anything to lose.

If you do take the challenge, I assure you, you will see the glory of God. You will come away with a bleeding heart full of the compassion of God. You will come back with a heavenly perspective; you will have a powerful testimony; but most of all, you will find yourself where Jesus already is. Remember again where Jesus said we would find Him? "I was hungry..., I was naked..., I was in prison..., I was sick..." We will make the glorious discovery that we will have been on mission with Jesus, for Jesus came "to seek and to save the lost" (Luke 19:10), not to create religious institutions and isolated saints. The command is to "go" not to "wait and hope they will come."

If you take this challenge, and if you want a team of men to go with you, then email me (wadeandkate@gmail.com). We already have a group, who have taken this challenge and have been forever changed. We will pray with you, fast with you, seek God's strategy, and go with you. It only takes you and another man to start a movement that could just take over an area for the glory of God.

The ball is in your court. Talk is cheap; it is time to step out of the boat; it is time to take the risk; it is time for action. Your life and my life are just too short to live any other way. Do you want to grow old and die without taking that risk? Do not let fear paralyze you; rather, throw it off and ask God to baptize your heart with His love. Friend, unlike William Booth and England in his day, God is bringing the nations to America. What a unique opportunity to not only see our cities impacted but also the nations impacted for the glory of God!!!

On with it, for the sake of Jesus and for the glory of God!!

APPENDIX A

Portland Rescue Mission Memory Verse

The Gospel
Set 1:

2 Corinthians 5:17
Philippians 1:6
1 Peter 2:23
John 16:24
John 14:21
1 John 1:3
Colossians 2:6
John 15.5
2 Timothy 2:15
Matthew 21:22
John 15:10,14
Acts 1:8

The Wheel
Set 2:

Romans 3:23
Romans 6:23
Hebrews 9:27
Romans 5:8
Ephesians 2:8,9
John 1:12,13
John 3:19
Romans 5:12
Romans 2:12
1 Peter 3:18
Romans 3:24
Revelation 3:20

Challenge
Set 1:

1 John 1:9
1 Peter 5:7
John 14:27
1 Corinthians 15:58
Romans 8:15-17
John 14:2,3
Ephesians 1:7
2 Corinthians 1:3,4
John 16:33
2 Corin. 5:10
1 Peter 1:3,4
Titus 2:12,13

Promised Blessings
Set 2:

Luke 9:23
2 Corin.6:17,18
James 1:12
Philippians 1:29
Ephesians 6:10,11
John 20:21
1 John 2:6
Romans 12:2
1 Corinthians 16:13
1 Peter 4:12,13
2 Timothy 2:3,4
Mark 16:15

Resources	**Expected Fruit**
Set 1:	**Set 2:**
Romans 8:14	Gal. 5:22,23
2 Peter 1:3,4	Acts 27:25
2 Timothy 1:7	John 15:11
John 8:31, 32	1 Corin. 10:13
Acts 2:25	Hebrews 10:36
1 Corin. 1:4,5	Phil. 2:3,4
1 Corin. 2:12	1 John 3:23
Romans 6:13	Hebrews 11:6
Ephesians 3:20	Philippians 4:4
James 1:5	1 John 4:4,5
Hebrews 13:5	James 1:2-4
2 Corin. 9:8	Col. 3:13,14

APPENDIX B

Elijah Generation Boot Camp for Young Men

Three days of re-training the spirit, mind, and body. Establishing a godly lifestyle, replacing the bad with what is right, the path of self-destruction with the path of life and righteousness.

The book of Proverbs is God's manual for a fatherless generation (23 times "My son" is spoken). See document <u>Proverbs – God's manual for young men for living godly and wisely in an age of sin and foolishness</u>

Areas to be addressed-

Morning to Night-

1. How to have a quiet time (i.e. – prayer closet, Word, and personal worship)

2. Make your bed, establishing order in your room and with your possessions

3. Personal hygiene (Shower, brushing teeth, combing hair, how to dress appropriately, personal appearance).

4. Giving of thanks before you eat

5. Proper table manners

6. Servant-heartedness (cleaning up/ serving without being asked).

7. Physical exercise and its importance (addressing hard work vs. laziness).

8. Diet/ sugar intake and its importance (taking care of God's temple)

9. Overcoming challenges/ trials/ fears vs. resorting to depression/ anger/ and defeat.

10. The importance of an education
11. The power of your words
12. The power of leading vs. following the crowd
13. Statistics – what do they say? What are you going to do about it?
14. Being a good steward of time (addressing addiction to video games and other time wasters).
15. Relating to girls. Proper conduct and improper conduct/ words and attitudes towards them.
16. The importance of good sleep
17. What it means to be a disciple, a <u>talmid,</u> of Jesus. Biblical understanding of discipleship.

** A rite of passage **
(token – necklace with a shield of faith and Joshua 1:9)

Can you stand alone? How are you going to react when temptations of violence, drugs, alcohol, sex, pornography, and other things come your way?

Replacing bad habits with good ones (television, music, video games, food, etc.)

Mentorship – One father/ mentor to a child, or one mentor to two kids.

Community – The power of a shared experience and initiation together (ex. Sports, African culture)

— Rite of Passage Group Confession —
Heavenly Father, I acknowledge You as my Father. I know that You are love, You are good, You are trustworthy, and You are

holy. I surrender to You today. I declare my faith and trust is in Jesus. He alone is my salvation; His blood alone can cleanse me and make me righteous in Your eyes. I surrender to your lordship. Jesus is Lord! I give my life to You.

I repent from all sins that I have committed with my eyes, my mouth, my mind, and my body and anything I have allowed in my heart that is not of You. I forgive all that have sinned against me, as You have forgiven me. I renounce all sin, whether pride, hatred, fear, lust, cursing, or hurting others in word and action, for against You and You only have I sinned. I renounce all the works of Satan in my life. I submit everything to You, Jesus, and I resist all satanic influence in my life now in Jesus' Name. Leave me and do not return. I ask now, Father, that You fill every area of my heart, soul, mind, and body. I give my eyes to You; let them see what You want me to see. I give my ears to You; let them hear what You want me to hear. I give my mind to You; let me think what You want me to think. I give my tongue to You, let me speak what You want me to speak. I give my body to You; let it be used in the way that glorifies You.

Baptize me, consume me, and fill me with Your Holy Spirit. I want to be Your vessel. Help me, teach me, and show me what it means to love You with all my heart, soul, mind, and strength and to love my neighbor as myself. Fill me with Your love. Give me revelation of who You are and Your great love for others and me. I break off all curses from my life and now receive the Father's blessing. Thank You, Father, for answering this prayer.

Thank You for Your love for me; I receive it now in Jesus' Name. Guide me now on paths of righteousness for Your namesake. Give me boldness to live for You and not ever be ashamed of You. You said that if I confess You, You will confess me, but if deny You,

You will deny me. Glorify Yourself through me! Make me one with You! Make me ready for the day that I stand before You and give an account of my life. I want to hear You say, "Well done, good and faithful servant. Enter into Your rest." I love You, Father! I pray all of this in Jesus' Name! Amen

<u>Schedule</u>

<u>Saturday-</u>

7:30 - Meet at JPM and begin to load up bags and food.

8:00 - Depart for Arrowhead

10:15 - Arrive at Arrowhead

10:30 - Introduction of schedule/ weekend- hooking up with kids and adult leaders- put bags away in cabin

11:00 - Event (Scavenger hunt/ race) (out and about to discover the property).

12:30 - Lunch (clean up assignments, teaching moment on table manners)

1:30 - Event (half of group does rock wall. Half does canoeing).

3:00 - Session #1 – IDENTITY IN CHRIST; SPLIT IN TWO GROUPS Elliot and Mike teaching

4:00 - Event (half of group does rock wall, half does canoeing)

5:30-6:00 - Rest, get ready for dinner

6:15 - Dinner (teaching moment on healthy food vs. sugary snacks).

7:00 - Session #2 -properly relating to girls. Geoff -

8:30 - Campfire (teaching moments)

9:30 - Lights out

Sunday-

6:30-7:00 - Breakfast

7:00-7:30 - Quiet time

7:45-8:15 - Individual instruction of personal hygiene

8:30-10:00 - Corporate Worship, Word (Session #3: Hard work vs. laziness) Bob Bauer and Prayer (teaching moment on importance of community)

10:00-12:00 - Event #4 (Hike -outdoor exploration).

12:30 - Lunch (assignments).

1:15-2:15 - Session #4 - emphasize power to overcome and grace! Geoff teaching to middle schoolers.

2:15-4:30 - Event (Half Archery and half rifle practice, then switch)

4:30-6:30 - Hayride, camp games (Capture the Flag), team building games.

6:45-7:30 - Dinner (teaching moment)

8:00 9:30 - Camp fire (Session #5: ANGER, REVENGE VS. LOVE, MERCY, INCLUDED IS HUMILITY VS. PRIDE) Bruce is teaching this session to all.

Monday-

6:30-7:00 - Breakfast

7:00-7:30 - Quiet time

7:30-8:15 - Individual words of wisdom, prayer and testimony from leaders to youth

8:30-9:45 - Session #5: PATH OF THE WICKED VS. PATH OF RIGHTEOUS, BOLDNESS, DISCIPLESHIP AS JESUS DEFINES IT. Rite of Passage, Laying on of hands, corporate response prayer, Pass out necklaces, final challenge.

9:45-10:15 - Clean up, pack up, and hit the road

12:15 - Arrive back at JPM.

** Bring journals to pass out for personal journaling (keeping
it simple!)

** Buy T-shirts?

** Get a couple of guys to be photographers, get action shots,
shots with individual leaders, group photo.

** Use two groups, 7-11 and 12-17

Keep sessions testimonial in nature

Dear parent(s),

We want to let you know of an awesome event that is coming up in April that your son can be a part of. We are taking a group of boys up to Camp Arrowhead next to Tuxedo, North Carolina (south of Asheville) for a weekend of challenges, encouragement, and, we believe, a life-changing experience. We will be splitting the boys into two age groups, 7-11 and 12-17. Currently, there are about twelve boys invited to this time, with twelve adults chaperoning (a background check on each chaperone is required. This allows them to be among those approved for volunteer service for Jackson Park Ministries). The facility is great, we will be able to kayak on a lake, do archery, use a rock-climbing wall, and we might even be able to include rifle practice for the older ones. It is beautiful acreage, and we will no doubt be spending some time exploring the woods and walking in and near the creek. We will be sleeping in cabins that have hot water for showers and have mattresses for us to sleep on (we will not be roughing it too muchJ). We will be providing the food; the kitchen facility is great for all uses. Most importantly, though, we will be emphasizing, "What does it mean to walk with the Lord and be His disciple?" We will also be covering the importance of every aspect of their lives, including personal hygiene, orderliness, education, relationships, physical exercise, and spending quality time with the Lord. We will be emphasizing the book of Proverbs and its practical instruction for wisdom in living. We will have a "rite of passage" at the end where we will encourage them to see themselves as responsible young men who are going to be leaders and not followers (by not giving into to bad peer pressure) in their generation. There are many who are already praying for this time. We are full of anticipation for what God has in store for them. The cost of the trip will be about $50.00; we as a ministry are willing to pay $35.00, so we are asking that you would please pay $15.00. The dates of the weekend are April 5th to the 7th (the 7th being the beginning of CMS's spring break). We are planning to leave Saturday morning and return Monday before lunch. We will seek to encourage the youth to set a little money aside for this trip, with your permission; from allowances you may give them (just $2.00 a week and they would have enough to pay for the trip).

Thank you for allowing us to invest in your son, we are believing that God is moving in his life, and this weekend could be very memorable for them—for the rest of their lives.

Cordially,

Wade McHargue
Youth/ Children's Pastor
Jackson Park Ministries

APPENDIX C

My Dream The Other Night

I dreamt I was watching, from a short distance away, men building a bridge across a great chasm. I knew in my heart that it would not be strong enough. I watched as they brought in a machine to work on the bridge. The weight of the machine caused the bridge to break, with all the steel, cement, and building materials crashing down into the chasm. I could sense the panic in the air as men scrambled about, trying to rescue the men who had fallen into this pit. I, with some others who I knew to be Christians, ran to help. The man who had driven the machine was trapped under the massive amount of debris. Somehow I was able to feel everything this man was feeling—it was utter panic. While trapped in the darkness around him, he increasingly realized he would soon run out of air to breathe if he was not rescued. <u>He was buried alive</u>! As I went down with others into the pit, I felt the presence of fear and death on this man. There were Christians looking for him at a middle level of the debris, but I knew that this man was much further down. I kept hearing in my dream, "Do unto others as you would have them do to you," and knew it applied to this buried man. I would want someone to go to all lengths to search for me, tirelessly, until they found me. I put my ear down to the ground and could hear muffled cries, but it was hard to discern where they were coming from. The other Christians who were with me searched and searched, but it seemed that they came to a place of giving up and retired from their search. I continued down further, and the mound of debris was very unstable; it was as if it was going to give way again. There was a very real risk of dying. I put my ear to the ground again; I could hear that the cries for help were getting weaker. There was an urgency because time was running out. Again, it was as if I could feel this man's panic. He was experiencing the horrid feeling that death was coming fast and the utter fear of not knowing what to expect, but with the knowledge that it would soon be over. I could feel the terror on this man. As I was pulling away boards and debris, I suddenly pulled away what was like the top of a coffin. In this utter darkness was the man. I grabbed his arm and pulled him out.

I asked God for the interpretation to this dream and I believe He spoke clearly. The bridge is man's effort to reach God, his effort to fulfill his destiny and to find life's meaning and purpose. Eventually, it will crash into the pit of sin, and all will be buried in their own lies. Buried alive, but as good as dead; alive, but dead in their own sins, awaiting the coming judgment and the second death. The message and unction from God was that we are to go and seek the lost. As I went down into the pit in my dream, I heard at least twice, "do unto others as you would want them to do to you." I had never thought of this verse in regards to evangelism. It hit me, as I was able to feel this man's panic and the imminent feeling of death, "What if that was me? To what degree would I want someone to come seek me out?" The other Christians looked for the man, but only to a point; then they gave up. I felt like God was challenging me, to what level am I willing to go? Would I risk my life? How far into the recesses of sin and wickedness am I willing to go to "rescue" a soul, by going after them in prayer and in preaching the Gospel? Where am I willing to go to reach them? There is a tremendous sense of urgency, that time is short and soon it will be too late. I have no fear of death; I have the answer, so why do I hesitate? May the Lord give us strength to go wherever He leads, to reach all for whom He suffered and died. O God, help us to place ourselves in their shoes with no fear, only boldness with Your love. Help us to reach out to the most wicked in the darkest pit, knowing that soon it could be too late. Let us reach them in the same way we would want someone to reach us.

God, help me and help Your church to be like Jesus and to seek and save that which is lost

Though I speak with the tongues of men and of angels, but have not love, I have become sounding brass or a clanging cymbal. And though I have the gift of prophecy, and understand all mysteries and all knowledge, and though I have all faith, so that I could remove mountains, but have not love, I am nothing. And though I bestow all my goods to feed the poor, and though I give my body to be burned, but have not love, it profits me nothing.

Love suffers long and is kind; love does not envy; love does not parade itself, is not puffed up; does not behave rudely, does not seek its own, is not provoked, thinks no evil; does not rejoice in iniquity, but rejoices in the truth; bears all things, believes all things, hopes all things, endures all things. Love never fails.

1 Corinthians 13:1-8

Acknowledgements

I want to thank and acknowledge:

My heavenly Father, my Lord Jesus, and the Blessed Holy Spirit. Thank you for saving me and giving me a reason to live. I live for You and for the glory of Your Name. May this book bring a smile to Your face and joy to Your heart and be used to mobilize Your "Elijah Generation." May you see an obedient life in this child of Yours. I love You.

My precious and beautiful wife Kate, whose faithful companionship, unconditional love, and humble servant-heartedness never ceases to challenge and minister to me. Your prayers, I know, have carried me further than I'll ever know this side of heaven. I am honored to be your husband. Proverbs 31:29.

My three amazing children. Abigail you are truly your "Father's joy." You are such a beautiful young woman of God (inside and out). God has given you so many gifts; I am excited to see how you will continue to use them to bring glory to Him. I pray, if it is God's will that you marry, that you will marry a man that exemplifies the attributes this book describes. Caleb, "bold one," my fellow warrior, may you continue to walk in holy conviction, love, humility, and power as you bear the torch for your generation to prepare the way for the return of Jesus. I know you and your brother will model the attributes of the "Elijah Generation" (you already are!). Josiah, whose "foundation is of God," you will run with your brother and fulfill God's call on your life, and there is no doubt in my mind that it is a great calling.

Dad and Mom. Thank you for your prayers, your patience, and your blessing (both those blessings you have spoken over me and those you have prayed into my life). Thank you for the freedom and encouragement you gave me to follow God's calling, through the thick and the thin, through the mountaintops and the valleys.

My two sisters, Lauren and Ashley, for your love and friendship. I thank God for your lives! I praise God for the men of God you have married.

Pastor Hartsell, for preaching the Gospel that I might be able to believe and be saved.

Pastor Deal, for modeling the spirit of Elijah long before I knew how to articulate this book. You have been a mentor to me, and the prophetic words God has spoken through you are coming to pass. I can never repay you for the faith-filled prayers to God that you have spoken for my family and me. I am deeply indebted to you.

Pastor Romoser, for your encouragement and even giving me pulpit time when I was just a youth. Thanks for believing in God's calling on my life. (And of course for marrying my wife and I!)

Pastor Leonard and Faith Tabernacle. I know you understand that we are never to despise the small beginnings. Thank you for looking past color and loving me with the love of Jesus. I will never forget my baptism! Thank you for pouring into my life!

Moody Bible Institute. Thanks for a great education and experience.

Dr. Michael Brown, for your pouring into my life and thousands of others. You are a great example of a true Talmid of Yeshua, and another who models the spirit of Elijah.

Pastor Kelvin, for your godly example and faithful encouragement. I am blessed to be a part of the family at SCCC!

My brothers from the Gatherings, what great things God has done in our lives! Memories that are forever sealed in our hearts and minds by the Spirit of God. May God grant us more together before we cross over into Glory. I look forward to living out the "Proposal" with you!

All who have faithfully stood with me and my family, those who sent us and kept us by your prayers and financial support in Guinea Bissau to see the discipleship center become a reality. How many times have I wished I could just embrace you and cry on your shoulder? Look at what great things God has done: tens of thousands preached to and so many, many lives surrendering to Jesus. Only God could open such wide doors of ministry!

To all those who now stand with us to see the Lakota know God's amazing, redeeming love for them, thank you!

Lafe Wood, for being a man of excellence in everything and for editing this book. I thank God for you brother!

Everyone else who has poured into my life and has been a friend through the years. You know who you are; I love you and thank God for you.

FOOTNOTES

[FOOTNOTE FOR PAGE 8]

*The 10/40 Window refers to the global land mass between ten and forty degrees north latitude where 82 percent of the world's poor reside and where 84 percent of the lowest quality of life exists (i.e., lowest life expectancy, highest infant mortality rate, and lowest literacy rate). It is estimated that 1.6 billion people have never had even one opportunity to hear the Gospel of Jesus Christ! Two thirds of the world's population lives in the 68 nations comprising the 10/40 Window. (For more information see <u>Operation World</u> by P. Johnson.)

[FOOTNOTE FOR PAGE 21]

*I would strongly recommend to anyone that they read "Living on Target" by Kelvin Smith, that addresses this Biblical order so articulately.

[FOOTNOTE FOR PAGE 108]

*I would like to add that I believe the "covering" spoken of in these verses does not have to be a cloth covering, for the Scriptures say that a woman's hair is given to her for a covering.

NEED ADDITIONAL COPIES?

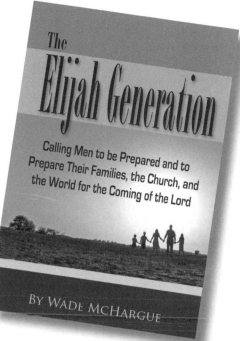

To order more copies of
The Elijah Generation,
contact NewBookPublishing.com

- ❑ Order online at:

  NewBookPublishing.com/Bookstore

- ❑ Call 877-311-5100 or

- ❑ Email Info@NewBookPublishing.com

Reliance
Media